"Richard has much experience in how to understand and activate chakras. Based on his experience, he wrote this spiritual book. I trust it can help people succeed in attaining healthy, harmonious interactions, and furthermore, achieve spiritual evolution.

To activate chakras in subtle energy (physical) dimensions, and to awaken chakras in spiritual dimensions, in a right way, is very important for keeping the body, mind, and spirit in healthy balance."

Hiroshi Motoyama, Ph.D., Ph.D.
Founder, California Institute for Human Science (CIHS)

"I CAN RELATE is an excellent book of great importance, and reading it was an enjoyable and enlightening experience. It is about our individual, inter-dimensional chakras, plus observed case-study consequences for dominant chakra pairings in major interpersonal relationships.

Dr. Jelusich provides perhaps the clearest and most useful teaching I have seen about the profound importance of understanding chakras to understand relationships. I strongly recommend this book for all of us in search of truth about ourselves as individuals, and as an enlightened species."

William A. Tiller, Ph.D.
Professor Emeritus, Stanford University
Dr. Tiller is in the film "What the Bleep Do We Know!?"

"Once again Dr. Jelusich offers very relevant information about subtle energy systems for readers interested in this important area of human functioning. He draws from extensive work in the field to illustrate practical ways of understanding how chakras reflect the dynamics of all human interaction, and he provides valuable strategies to develop healthy interpersonal relationships."

Elizabeth Newby-Fraser, Ph.D.
Dean of Psychology, California Institute for Human Science

"Dr. Jelusich is the real deal. He has a powerful ability to see through the layers of who we think we are (as individuals and in relationships), to the real essence of our core, our spirit, and our psychology. In this follow-up to his ground-breaking Eye of the ⸻ s: Psychology of the Chakras, he continues his profound in⸻ chakras and their effects on modern hum⸻ is an eye-opener...*a must read.*"

I CAN RELATE

*How we intuitively choose
the people in our lives*

(follow-up to EYE OF THE LOTUS: *Psychology of the Chakras*)

Richard Jelusich, Ph.D.

LIGHT
NEWS
PUBLISHING

Editing by *Karyn L. Wilkening*
Expert Editing, Ink, San Diego, CA

Illustrations and layout by *Michael Brouillet*
Kaleidoscope Creative, BC, Canada

Dr. Jelusich's photo by *Carolina Van Leeuwen*
Van Leeuwen Photography, Encinitas, CA

I CAN RELATE
How we intuitively choose the people in our lives
Printed in Canada and USA
First printing: September, 2008
ISBN: 978-0-9818634-0-5

Light News Publishing
P.O. Box 17035, San Diego, CA 92177
Toll free: 877-242-5721
www.lightnews.org

This book is dedicated to my mother,
Lena Philomena Jelusich,
who at this writing is 90 and thriving.
She is a remarkable woman,
possessed of noble and gentle qualities
too numerous to mention.
Her eloquence and stature, I hope,
flows through my efforts to help people understand their
spiritual natures and recognize their true selves.

Maybe she wishes I had stayed an engineer,
or was rooted in some more established practice.
But it is necessary for me to voyage into
the wondrous workings of the soul and its yearning
for perfect symmetry and pureness
of love and compassion.

As our souls relate as mother and son,
I have been inspired by her ideals, and I aspire
to achieve in this lifetime some of the great
qualities she represents.

I love you, Mom.
Thank you for being the virtuous
Soul that you are.
You are a continuing inspiration to me.

ACKNOWLEDGEMENTS

To incept a work based on intuition
I remind myself that I am only the instrument,
and my gratitude goes to the Creator for my life's path.

I appreciate all who have inspired and urged me to write,
and espically those dedicated professionals who helped
craft, design, and edit this book.

Thank you to my dear Mary, who has shared her heart,
given her selfless counsel, and taught me valuable
things about myself.

Thanks to my children and their families for being among
my greatest teachers. I can see in our interactions that which
is mirrored in this book.

And I wish to acknowledge those individuals in the many
case histories. Their dominant chakras and interpersonal
dynamics illustrate how the process of "relationship"
is an unfolding, evolving dance of
perception/reaction/awareness.

CONTENTS

I CAN RELATE

WHEN READING THIS BOOK

Your relationship with others exists on many levels. Some of the most difficult and challenging are those relationships that are intimate or familial.

Taking an *energetic relationship* to each other is something we all do ceaselessly, whether we know it or not, whether we believe it or not. Most people are not aware that we are qualitatively tuned in to each other on many levels all the time, and that the conscious mind is last to realize what is really going on.

Ninety-five percent of all communication is energy. It is neither verbal nor physical, but a linking of consciousness between people. Most of what is really going on is at a higher level of consciousness, and that constructs the framework of the interactions of the mind/heart at the lower waking levels of consciousness. Ninety-five percent is not a static number; it's meant to imply that *most* of what is going on with us and between us is on much higher, more elevated level of our Selves.

One of the purposes of this book is to help you awaken higher sense-perceptions that you already have. Another purpose is to show, through many case examples, how the real psychic interaction works between people, causing you to have more awareness of your own consciousness through your energy centers – *your chakras.*

There is a seamless connection between all the chakras; we just tend to dwell more in one for the benefit of our life's experiences that develop the nature of our character through our free-will choices.

All of our chakras are working. Even though we may be

dominant in one, the rest are fully functioning. So, you may experience attributes in your Self, or reflected back to you in others, that are triggered by moving into the consciousness of various chakras that may not be the dominant one.

Understanding the *motivation* of another person is the key to understanding the current of energy underlying the relationship. Knowing their dominant chakra will help you to understand their desires, strengths, weaknesses, and disposition towards life. This knowing is intended to help you build strong, meaningful and productive relationships. It is meant to emphasize the positive aspects and minimize the negative aspects of one's behavior.

The old saying goes: "If you want to change your mate, change yourself." That means you must change your Self if you wish to seek changes in your relationships. *Nothing will change unless you do.* It has to do with the Hermetic Law of Cause and Effect. Unless you change the cause, you'll continue to achieve the same effect.

The Chinese say: "Unless you change the road you're on, you're bound to end up where you're headed!" And Gandhi said: "We must *be* the change we seek in the world." He did not say *become* and he did not say *intend.* Change requires *action.* Sometimes, you have to get up off your intention and do something. In the case of relationships, if you are waiting for someone in your life to change, you may have a very, very long wait.

It is my hope that the information here will help you to better understand the workings of the *whole human being.* That is, all four archetypes that imbue us with the qualities of being human, including our metaphysical nature. They are: mental, physical, spiritual, and emotional states of being. These four archetypes must flow together in congruity in a symphony of motion for you to know health, optimal living, and true self-empowerment. Such is the basis of living an authentic life, overcoming the illusions of separation, and overcoming suffering. All healing, no matter what type it is, always boils down to one thing:

> *Healing is overcoming any illusion*
> *that separates you from the Oneness*
> *in which you already live.*

Remember, you are in charge of your life and you have choices. You are made in the image of the Creator - composed of all Will, Love and Wisdom - *whole and complete.*

Author's Note

I have put off publishing this book for way too long. If you read its predecessor, <u>Eye of the Lotus: *Psychology of the Chakras*</u>, there was mention that the title of this follow-up book was to be <u>The Book of Reciprocity</u>. I realized it was unwieldy and difficult to, ah, *relate* to, so I changed the title to the friendlier <u>I Can Relate</u>.

As you may have noticed, we are in a cycle where everything is rapidly accelerating, from time to consciousness. There is now greater possibility for imbalance in our world. Never before in the recent epoch has humanity experienced such an abundance of information and the rapidity of its delivery from every direction. And yet, technological advances have not improved the evolution of the "whole human being" as self-realized spiritual beings symbiotic with the material world, nor helped humanity to live in balance.

The reason I write books, teach spiritual healing, take groups to study the Maya, and more, is that our *spirituality is all related to balance, and to how we make the effort to hold that balance.* It is so crucial that we do so in these times.

As Goethe said: "Where the Light is great, the Shadow is deep." Never in this epoch have we had such opportunity for inner growth and utter destruction. We must choose wisely, with compassion and harmlessness, if we are to evolve to a higher level of our Selves.

You'll find this book easy to read, even though it deals with higher aspects of your Self, the quality and affect of the chakra system on your consciousness, and your interactions/relationships with others throughout life.

I cover the basics of the chakra system and its psychology and reciprocity, how to determine the dominant chakra for your Self and those around you, how we take energetic relationships to each other, and many case histories to show how one chakra dominant individual can take a relationship to another chakra dominant individual, the potential strengths and weaknesses and how that energetic interaction plays out. In reading the case histories, you'll gain a deeper understanding of how the energetic dynamics unfold.

This book will deal with the chakric relationships between people with respect to chakras 2 through 6, leaving chakras 1 and 7 out. The reason is that chakras 1 and 7 are more like gateways to existence, which do not have as much effect upon the waking consciousness of the individual as chakras 2 through 6.

For ease of reading, numbers are used in the text to represent a chakra dominant person. For example:

2 = 2nd chakra = Second Chakra Dominant Person

3 = 3rd chakra = Third Chakra Dominant Person

4 = 4th chakra = Fourth Chakra Dominant Person

An example of the text might be: "When a 2 meets a 3, the reciprocity of the two people is ...."

In addition, when using reference chakras, the captioning will look like this:

5-2 = Fifth Chakra Dominant Person with a reference to their Second Chakra

3-4 = Third Chakra Dominant Person with a reference to their Fourth Chakra

An example of the text might be: "When a 4-3 is engaging with a fully 3, they can have a tendency to behave like a 3, but really be masking their true nature as a 4."

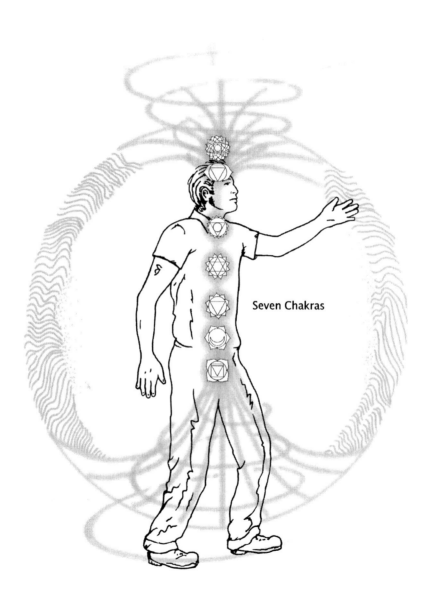

Seven Chakras

FORWARD

How do we relate to others? What is the process by which we bring people into our lives who are the reflections of our inner desires for balance? Is it merely by chance, or is there some aspect that ensures everyone we meet is in some way a reflection of God, and of our Selves? Is there more to it than merely making our way through life with what we know?

The process by which two or more people engage energetically is dynamic (in movement) and ceaseless. It is a dance of consciousness, making a symphony of connections that eventually surface as an opinion or feeling. We compose our opinions based on the myriad belief systems that cover our true wants and desires, which are covering our soul's purpose.

Many times what we think we want and desire is a process of those belief systems, colored by the perceptions of what we feel we lack (rooted in the illusion of separation from the Oneness). Hence, we often look for others who help complete us, whether that is a wholesome experience or not. Throw in a dose of morals and ethics and you have the script for a play with many complex undertones.

No wonder relationships sometimes leave us wondering why we even have them! I believe many of us have wondered just what the dynamics are in our relationships that can leave us so dazed and confused. Certainly, none of you have ever had this problem, right? Right.

The two strongest forms of karma in relationship are parental karma and familial karma. Parental karma is you

Every person has
one chakra that
is more dominant
than the others.

and your parents and you and your children. Familial karma is your marriage, siblings, and other family ties. It is here that we experience the deepest forms of relationships, partly because they can be long term, but mostly because of the attachment (karma, good or bad) that we have for these relationships.

Continuing where Eye of the Lotus left off, we are going to cover how every person has one chakra that is more dominant than the others, affecting their mental, emotional, physical, and spiritual states of being, and how that chakra-dominant person takes an energetic relationship to other people, both casual and intimate.

As you may recall, chakras are energy centers in the body that regulate the flow of life-force (consciousness) between dimensions. They are us, our higher organs, and are our link to higher levels of our own existence.

There is an energy disposition underlying the motivation and interaction in our relationships. Chakric relationships apply to all. Many who read this book may find the most value when applying what you learn to your own family - mom and dad, you and your spouse, your children, and so on.

Spirituality, no matter which chakra, is always about balance. There is duality in everything, and our chakras are at once our challenge and our strength. It is not about the balance itself, but about the effort you make to hold that balance. The effort you expend is what defines the nature of your character in a lifetime. We must always strive to remain in balance.

I've provided a little guide to determine which chakra might be dominant in you and those you are concerned with, so that you can observe your interactions from an informed place, and thus strengthen your relationships. Spouses, partners, and parents may find this information especially helpful, but it can also be useful for friends, employers and employees, co-workers, and just about anyone who has a relationship with someone else.

Language and culture are not barriers. Everyone has a dominant chakra, so if you are interacting with someone from another country/culture, the elements described here still apply.

Consciousness is a dance, always unfolding and changing. Knowing how the dance unfolds allows you to step through life in tune with your fellow souls more elegantly and with greater benefit to all. As you are more self-empowered spiritually and awaken your higher sense-perceptions, so also are you able to help more people achieve their self-empowerment as well.

My purpose in offering a number of case histories and examples is to place many real-life events before you that may be familiar or similar to your experience, and also to expose you to some that are as yet unfamiliar.

You may see a little of your Self in many of the examples because the consciousness of all of our chakras is seamlessly working together as one. But we do tend to differentiate into one particular chakra more than the others, which sets our perceptions of the universe and our initial reactions to our relationship encounters.

If you know that everyone you meet is a reflection of the God within you, it will only help you to have a better understanding of your Self. There is an old saying: "If you ever want to know how your life is going, look at the friends you keep." If you wish to change your friends, you must first change you.

When you understand how the energetics of consciousness works through your dominant chakra, you become self-empowered and self-determined.

FORWARD

CHAPTER 1

WHEN FIRST WE MEET

We understand what it is to regard someone when we first meet - we size them up, taking in mostly visual information and matching it with our inner emotional and mental criteria, based on however many years of existence we've currently had on this planet (called the "experiential set").

Did you ever hear that we usually know in the first four seconds of meeting someone pretty much how we feel about them - that we've sized them up and that summation determines how we will treat and respond to them? Imagine the minutiae the human mind is capable of retaining and processing; so many billions of bits of subtle and not-so-subtle cues from those people we encounter. Imagine coming to a bottom line in just a few seconds about someone you may spend the rest of your life with!

About fifteen years ago, an article in the San Diego newspaper about astronomers and their observations of the universe stated that the visual universe, the one we can see, is about 10% of the total of what's out there. The other 90%, they said, is composed of "all other dark matter."

Would you make up your mind about someone based on the 10% that you *see*? And yet we do it all the time! There is another universe, above this one, in which you and I are already members. But it cannot be perceived with thoughts, the physical mind, or the five senses. It must be perceived through inner trust and faith of the feeling state of our being.

We may think this higher universe is above and separate from the one in which our five senses live most of this lifetime. The truth is that both universes occupy the same space at the same time; we are just unaware that such elegant universes exist, within us.

PERCEPTION/WILL/REACTION

The law of cause and effect states that until we change or realize the cause, we will always achieve the same effect. Why then, can we not prevent some lessons or reflections of others from coming into our lives? Why can we not just reason it out? *Because awareness has nothing to do with thinking.*

Awareness is a state of being from which the thoughts of the mind flow, not the other way around. The only way to overcome an illusion is to first recognize there is one. That sounds like a circular argument, but it is true.

With a higher quality of awareness comes a different perspective. You begin to understand why you do the things you do; why you bring people into your life to reflect back certain qualities to you.

We perceive, and then through the power of our will, we react. When you perceive more accurately, more fully, your reactions will change.

One of the really great things about being a human being is that we have a free will to choose. As we become more aware, the illusions of our life show up and present themselves

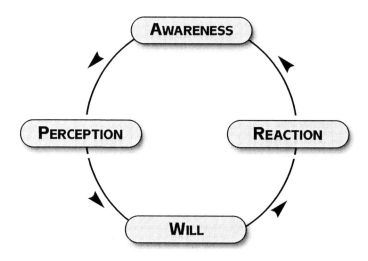

as *Well, are you going to keep doing the same thing, or are you going to evolve beyond this?*

As you make the effort to evolve, to live a productive and meaningful life in harmlessness, you also live in the dharma that allows you to ascend to higher levels of awareness in the quality of your character, freeing your perspective to see things and people as they are, not as they appear.

If you know the dominant chakra of another person, if you apply these principles, what you are really doing is awakening higher sense-perceptions in your Self. You are empowering your Self to be a more aware, more conscious being who can choose your reactions.

THE FIRST LEVEL OF ENCOUNTER – THE MIND

Of course, the mind is the first level of encounter *that our minds believe is occurring,* when in reality the more elegant part of our nature already has established the psychic connection

3

through the feeling (intuitive) state. The first level is what our mind initially believes is the only level – how we think and act, how another person appears, his or her demeanor, appearance, sex, sexuality, race, culture and ethnicity, and so on.

We base these decisions on our experiential set; how our own experiences have helped shape our ideas of the world and people. Our experiences with family, upbringing, intimate relationships, work, etc., have all shaped our outlook on life, and many of us assess new relationships based on how our prior relationships have gone.

This is a huge mistake, for it puts a severe limitation on the various possibilities the new relationship presents for growth and new understanding.

Especially in intimate relationships, it's best not to make assumptions on your new relationships from your old ones. Your feelings are always available, and in relationships many more women employ their use than do men.

It is natural for men in our culture to place an emphasis on visual and sexual cues. It is natural for women in our culture to place a high emphasis on verbal expressions and feelings (pre-emotions), and they are correct to do so. If we could all trust our feelings more from a standpoint of our seamless connection to our own higher Selves, that would be optimal.

It is true that most of us are unaware of our metaphysical nature, that we do size people up on what we know, what we've observed in life, our past experiences, our acculturation and all the many facets that our minds learn from living in the third dimension.

But what about your own higher nature? Doesn't it stand to reason that you're going to use your mental faculties, the same ones that have rooted you in the third dimension, to dominate your assessments? This is normal, and we can observe people following their hearts as they cast away reason and logic.

The mind or ego has a strong desire to be in control, and in the absence of the direct knowledge of our true nature, it is doing its best to make sense of this dimension of time and space.

The physical mind is so inured in this dimension that it knows of no other existence, but through that which we call feelings. And when I say feelings, I don't mean just those feelings tied solely to the emotions.

The difference between *feelings* and *emotions* is that a feeling is what comes to you, what you sense as a quality of being, but not a quantity like feeling the heat of the summer sun. *An emotion is what you do with a feeling.* An emotion is a feeling externalized or given action through your will.

A feeling is a higher sense-perception that is based on our seamless connection to All That Is. I like to use the term "God" but there are many associations. Semitic religions like Christianity, Judaism, and Islam refer to God as a being, perhaps with a personality. Asian religions like Buddhism and Hinduism see God as an Absolute, a Oneness, or Emptiness. We live in a Oneness regardless of your term to describe it. It is that seamless connection that allows us to feel what cannot be known by the physical mind.

The smallest feeling is greater than the greatest thought. When you feel someone's anger, it is the psychic phenomenon that you are experiencing first. The mind then takes in its visual and auditory assessments and mixes with the feelings/psychic nature to determine a response.

One of the greatest mistakes you could possible make is to underestimate who you truly are. If you really are of the Oneness, you are a part of all Will, Love, and Wisdom. That means that what you feel about someone in your life is going to be pretty accurate, but it is based on your power to trust your feelings, then apply what you know.

The problem is that we all do have the feeling capabilities I've described, but we gloss over those feelings with the grossness of mental presuppositions and materialistic orientations. Sometimes the person is "not who we thought they were." *Exactly.*

Relationships are dynamic and fluid. As you will see in the many case examples in this book, there are times when you can be doing everything right and still have the relationship not turn out well.

Remember that relationships are based on two free-will powers of choice, not just yours. You can be doing everything right and the other person can make other choices regardless, because of their free will.

THE SECOND LEVEL OF ENCOUNTER – THE TRUE EXPERIENCE

What if the person we meet is really a reflection of our own universe of desires, spiritual growth, and evolution? What if the person we meet has already been "scripted" into our lives on some higher level of our Selves, and that we are now just physically meeting him or her? What if this new encounter is another reflection of the God within? Or yet another externalization to balance the imbalance that is based on the illusion of separation?

The second level of encounter is the *psychic level.* This is the true experience, even though our minds believe the real encounter is of the physical mind only. In fact, the second level is really the first level, and actually the *only* level.

Once you understand that your psychic abilities are really the access to, and opening of, your own higher sense-perceptions, you also will understand that in using them you can perceive people as they really are. Then you can use your

WHEN FIRST WE MEET

mind to make further judgments *after* you trust your feelings.

This is most difficult to relate when one has no experience of its reality. Through history, various spiritual authors have sought to evoke our higher nature, but have had much difficulty. The reason is that the only way to truly know God is with a direct, revelatory experience. That is, you cannot know your higher Self unless you are vulnerable to that same higher part of you. No one can do it for you, and while the mind is very powerful, it alone is not enough to grasp the experience of this higher level of being.

What I tell my Healer's Training students is: "Trust what you feel, apply what you know." It means to trust your feelings *first*, then you can use the capabilities of the physical mind. You are sacrificing nothing of the physical mind; you are just putting the more eloquent form of your nature in practice first. Yes, it takes a huge amount of personal trust and faith in your own inner feelings, but the more fiercely you do so, the better the result. Your inner feelings (inner knower) are the conduit to All That Is.

If you recognize this as true and trust it, there is no higher guidance, but ever-unfolding higher levels of awareness.

You become more authentic and genuine: the difference between the mind's third-dimensional "stuck-ness" and the higher dimensional reality becomes less and less because you are overcoming the illusion of separation from the Oneness.

Eventually, your physical mind will become accustomed to the use of your higher sense-perceptions. Again, the more you trust in this process, the more you realize your true nature, the more empowered you are as a spiritual being and the more you will perceive people as they truly are.

That also means that your relationships have the opportunity to be profound because you are profoundly beholding the true nature of the other person, whether it is a family member, co-worker, or intimate partner.

It also means you may be transforming and transcending some of your relationships because you will understand their true basis and your part in it. With clarity comes the responsibility for your own right action, according to your moral and ethical code.

When you see people as they really are, you understand their true motivations *and* your part in the relationship.

CHAPTER 2

THE CASE FOR INTIMATE RELATIONSHIPS AND MARRIAGE

In times past, many gurus and yogis were against the idea of marriage. They felt that people should not join together if they thought that the other person would "complete" them or make them whole, for they believed if you live in a Oneness, no one can complete you but your Self. They advised that people would be wise to complete themselves first.

The idea of "soul mates" and "twin flames" is a much over-used and watered-down interpretation of great relationship soul matches. In the course of many years of spiritual counseling I have seen some relationships that were definitely and clearly meant to be, whether through karma or mission statements. I've also seen relationships that have run their course with partners hanging on in false hope of resolution.

The reality is *there are many so-called twin flames or soul mates for every person.* We tend to localize our feelings into our geography, age, culture, economy, and many other topical but limiting factors that cause us to make false assumptions,

precluding the possibility of great relationships arising from unexpected and perhaps irrelevant sources.

Fear of lack is the greatest selling tool ever invented. You see it all the time: "Sale ends today," or "Only a limited number of items on hand." The fear of lack extends deeply into our desire for meaningful relationships. "Will it last forever?" "Is he/she *the one*?" "Am I getting too old, and no one will be interested in me?" "If I'm not married by age XX, life is over." Don't laugh. I've heard these statements and many more based on fear of lack; that it's a limited universe and you have to get all you can, while you can.

So many people play this desperate game in relationships. Have a flat stomach, big breasts, large muscles, broad back, lots of money, handsome/pretty, and so on. Such a formula for suffering! All based on the idea of separation, when there is none. And *all* of this is based only on the 5% that is physical when the 95% of what is really going on is on a much higher level.

We tend to try to guarantee that our soul mate will show up by reading the latest how-to-attract your mate articles and stories, by having the right job, the right style, and so on. There are many who now use the Internet for matchmaking. If you truly believe the universe is infinite, do you also believe that a computer program can match you with someone better than your own inner magnet, your inner-knower, can? Perhaps. There's nothing wrong with using matching services for dates. But in the end you must recognize that your relationships are an externalization of your soul looking for balance and the true reflection of your inner Self, to overcome the illusion of separation.

In other words, you live in such an elegant universe that you could meet the most significant intimate relationship in your life at a local store quite by accident. The reason? It is that you are in constant psychic communication with all souls in all places; that you live in a Oneness where there is no separation, and that the persons most suitable for you are already in queue (call it an extra-dimensional queue, if you like) long before your conscious mind is ever aware of it.

Most of us are so used to pop culture instant gratification that we don't realize great matches take a long time to materialize, and that you may have to go through some necessary prior relationships to prepare you for the one that is long-term.

You are a part of many types of karma that help define the course of your life's experiences: individual, parent/child, family, soul group, city, etc. But along with that karma there is also your *dominant chakra disposition* setting your life's experiences and perceptions, and the way in which you attract your relationships, especially intimate relationships that lead to living together and marriage.

And yes, there are relationships that have been together through karma in past lives. I've seen many of them and when I do, I advise that this is a lifetime where they were to marry to experience the union of two loving souls once again. (Read about examples in the Case Histories section.)

In our more modern times, many of the yogis now feel that a marriage can provide a strong foundation for true spiritual growth, as long as each individual is strong in personal spiritual development.

Marriage forces you to make a commitment to your partner and to your Self. It is not the vows themselves, but the internal commitment that you make that helps define your character. It is also a commitment to your Self: that you are worthy of a great and profound loving relationship; that you are worthy of receiving as much love as you give; and that you can attract a perfect relationship into your life.

One of the greatest charges a minister can give to a couple

in a marriage ceremony is: "May you each retain a sense of your own individuality." Remember that when you are in a committed relationship, it is important for you to keep a sense of your own spiritual evolution, your uniqueness. The Buddhists would say: "You must empty your cup before you can fill it." In Buddhist philosophy that means you would spend a whole lifetime getting to know who you are, so that in the end you can let it all go!

Whether you are committing to another person on paper or in your heart, the relationship with your Self must first be sound and holy. You cannot have a great relationship with another person, be it intimate, familial, or otherwise, unless you are on good terms with your Self.

Two of the most powerful healing tools are *prayer* and *meditation*, by whatever name you evoke, within a divine guidance by which your trust your feelings, your inner knower that effortlessly guides you to the highest and fullest expression of your Self for your greatest good.

If you have spiritual practices, maintain them. If not, find a spiritual teacher whom you trust to help guide you to the externalization of your soul's desires. If your desire is a committed relationship such as marriage, it can provide you a profound, grounded and stable means of growing in dharma (right action, right behavior).

Prayer is talking to God.
Meditation is listening for the answer.

THE 7 CHAKRA LOCATIONS

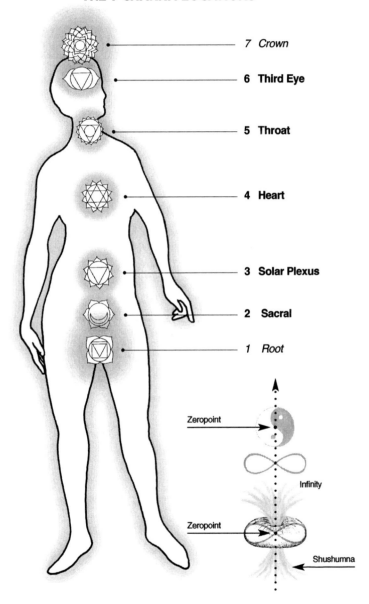

7 *Crown*

6 **Third Eye**

5 **Throat**

4 **Heart**

3 **Solar Plexus**

2 **Sacral**

1 *Root*

Zeropoint

Infinity

Zeropoint

Shushumna

A Chakra is a localized space-time continuum event, a toroidal energy field through which the archetypes of the emanations of consciousness enter the third dimension.

CHAPTER 3

A SHORT REVIEW OF CHAKRA TYPES

The chakras are our higher organs; our connection to a higher part of our existence that is still us, but a more eloquent expression of our soul and its true nature.

Everyone on the planet has chakras, but the number of people with *awakened* chakras is very few. We must work on our spiritual life in order to awaken our chakras.

The term "qualitative emanation" is not easy to understand, but it captures the essence of what our chakras really do. The phrase is like an oxymoron (two words put together that don't seem to belong together). How can you emanate a quality? Even though ironic, that is precisely what happens in consciousness. An emanation is similar to the radiation of light and heat from the sun. It spreads out its rays of influence in all directions at all times.

Instead of emanating light or something physically measurable, our chakras emanate consciousness that we all are attuned to in ourselves and others through our higher sense-perceptions. In this book you're learning that those senses exist and how we (mostly unconsciously) take psychic relationships to each other because of those qualitative emanations.

The chakras are inter-dimensional, localized space-time events, where the quality of our consciousness emanates into this dimension from higher dimensions of reality through seven main energy centers lined up with the column of the spine.

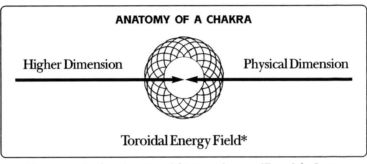

ANATOMY OF A CHAKRA

Higher Dimension   Physical Dimension

Toroidal Energy Field*

*For more indepth explanation of this term please read Eye of the Lotus.

The chakras are still you, just you on a higher level of your Self.

The chakras are our windows to our higher Selves, ceaselessly flowing the quality (not quantity) of our souls into our waking consciousness (personality) in this dimension. "Quality" refers to a state of being. A qualitative example would be: "Do you love your mother?" Responding in a resounding "yes" cannot be quantified; it is a quality, a state of being varying only in intensity of feeling, not thinking.

Qualitative emanation, then, is the property of each chakra to radiate your consciousness out in all directions, to all people.

Relationships are a function of this qualitative emanation flowing in both directions simultaneously between and among people. In intimate encounters, casual conversation or within a crowd, the essence of the qualitative emanations of one's consciousness is ceaseless.

The following two tables show the major chakras and their effects on the personality. Please note that this book, like its predecessor, <u>Eye of the Lotus</u>, emphasizes chakras 2 through 6 as those most affecting our daily waking consciousness, although all seven chakras are listed.

CHAKRA	NAME	SANSKRIT NAME
1	*Root*	*Muladhara*
2	**Sacral**	**Svadhisthana**
3	**Solar Plexus**	**Manipura**
4	**Heart**	**Anahata**
5	**Throat**	**Visuddha**
6	**Brow or Third Eye**	**Ajna**
7	*Crown*	*Sahasrara*

CHAKRA	NAME	CHARACTERISTIC	EFFECT
1	*Root*	*Survivability*	*Gateway to mere existence in physical form*
2	**Sacral**	**Creationist**	**Creativity, burdens, responsibility, sexuality, sensuality**
3	**Solar Plexus**	**Charismatic Leader**	**Power of the Self, individuation, truth**
4	**Heart**	**Empath**	**To be what love is; to give and receive love**
5	**Throat**	**Communicator**	**To articulate what humanity cannot yet understand; elucidation and illumination**
6	**Brow or Third Eye**	**Prophet**	**Higher communication; inception of new paradigms of being**
7	*Crown*	*Zero-Point*	*Gateway to higher dimensions*

We tend to be dominant in one chakra more than the rest, and this dominance seems to influence us for our whole lives. Although all of our chakras are open, we do tend to remain mostly in the influence of the given dominant chakra.

However, all our chakras affect us through consciousness at all times, and we have challenges in each many times over the course of our lives. For instance, you may be dominant in your fifth chakra as a communicator, but may have at one or more times had a money challenge (second chakra).

An easy way to picture this concept is as a lake of water that contains all the chakras. Perhaps the third chakra is the grassy area, the second a rocky bottom, the fourth a shallow area, and so on. You may be like a fish, freely able to swim to any part of the lake you wish (life issues), but you may prefer to hang out in one area (chakra) more than the rest.

It seems to be this way in life: we are disposed to hang out in a given dominant chakra disposition towards life, but may float to different chakras at various times because our consciousness is composed of all the chakras, all the time.

While you may be third chakra dominant and temporarily have a second chakra issue of money (abundance), you will eventually float back to your most dominant chakra, viewing life through your most familiar viewpoint or orientation. There is no seam between chakras, and we are composed of the totality of our consciousness.

Chakras 2, 4, and 6 tend to be more yin-type chakras: feminine (energy), receptive, nurturing, emotionally-based, enfolding.

Chakras 1, 3, 5, and 7 tend to be more yang-type chakras: masculine (energy), manifestative, assertive, progressive.

You can probably already guess what happens when a relationship mixes say a 2 and a 5, or a 3 and a 3, for example. Many of these relationships will be examined in the Case Histories section.

CHAKRA	NAME	DISPOSITION
1	*Root*	*Yang*
2	**Sacral**	**Yin**
3	**Solar Plexus**	**Yang**
4	**Heart**	**Yin**
5	**Throat**	**Yang**
6	**Brow or Third Eye**	**Yin**
7	*Crown*	*Yang*

EACH CHAKRA HAS A PSYCHIC ABILITY

Each chakra is a transformer, not only of energy but also of consciousness, in four archetypes (mental, physical, spiritual, emotional). Each chakra produces in the personality a psychic ability that is unique to that chakra. The table below outlines these psychic abilities.

CHAKRA	PSYCHIC ABILITY
2	Sees the true potential in others and in humanity
3	Incisiveness, cleaves truth from untruth
4	Empathy, sees the emotional potential in others
5	Telepathy and higher meaning/comprehension
6	Clairsentience and knowing of the higher paradigm

Our dominant chakras are part of a system of intuition; a finely-tuned network of intuition that is "on" 24/7 and affects the way we think, process information, and perceive our reality and relationships.

The dominant chakra, as seen in the table above, incepts that basic psychic ability in a myriad of variations on its basic power. You could have 100 people with a dominant 2nd chakra in a room, and not one of them will be the same. But they would have similar attributes, as colored by their 2nd chakra dominance.

HIGHER AND LOWER ASPECTS OF THE CHAKRAS

Below is a synopsis of each chakra and its higher and lower aspects. The aspect of a chakra refers to those attributes that a person may possess, but may or may not be present functionally in their lives. (Remember, we're concentrating on chakras 2 through 6.)

For example, the higher aspect of the 2 is to be the visionary/explorer, one who sees the big picture and presents it to humanity. The lower aspect of the 2 is to be the martyr/victim, one who loses faith or hope, spreads themselves too thin, etc.

CHAKRA	NAME	HIGHER ASPECT	LOWER ASPECT
2	The Creationist	The visionary. One who sees the big picture. The one who inspires others through a life of faith and trust, and sees the true potential in others.	The martyr, the victim, the workaholic who spreads too thin over multiple priorities. The life of chaos, one who is self-destructive, or vindictive and petty.
3	The Charismatic Leader	The giver of truth, the spiritual leader, the entrepreneur. One who helps emphasize virtue and individuation of the Self. One who stands in the authority and authenticity of Self.	The manipulator, or one who allows manipulation of Self. The procrastinator from one's power. Holds anger at life's inequities. Takes things personally.
4	The Empath	One who represents what love is, and who feels what others feel. True compassion and healing.	The human emotional pincushion. One who represents the absence of love.

CHAKRA	NAME	HIGHER ASPECT	LOWER ASPECT
5	The Communicator	The teacher. One who articulates for humanity what cannot yet be known. The nexus point, the networker and the catalyst. One who heals the mind.	The hermit, continuously ungrounded. Leads others into false awareness as the false prophet. Alone in a crowd.
6	The Prophet	One who incepts the new paradigm of being. Higher level communication and awareness.	Emotionally unattached, over analytical, and suffering from abstract thinking.

We can choose to be in the higher aspect of each chakra through our lives. But many times we are challenged by ourselves and others, placing us in the lower aspect(s) of a given chakra.

The lower aspects represent the challenges we must face in life in order to live fully in the higher aspects. The lower aspects are like going to the *chakra gym*: we must work out against the resistance of the lower aspect over and over until we gain strength from the challenge. This way, the next time we face that particular challenge, we would have developed the muscles of the will to meet the challenge, and overcome it.

The lower aspects of our chakras assure us that we will bring the people and circumstances into our lives to help facilitate the *balance* we seek, because those lower aspects are rooted in the illusion of separation. We are *guaranteed* to bring those events into our lives, because they represent the cures for our afflictions.

By our very nature we seek to bring those experiences into our lives that will develop our character, through our free-will choices, into more self-aware, self-empowered beings.

The reason is that everything tends toward perfection, and we always tend to externalize that search by bringing those relationships into our lives that will help us balance our Selves.

Meeting the resistance of the challenge enough times will help you to no longer be drawn to such challenges, as you will work within the law of cause and effect to change the cause, thus achieving a different effect. Once you achieve balance in one lesson, you go on to another.

TO DO - TO LEARN

What we have come "to do" and "to learn" are two different things - two sides of the same coin that are simultaneously served as we live our life to its best exposition through our free will. The table below explains the To Do - To Learn for dominant chakras 2 through 6.

The characteristics are driven by the incarnation of the personality (our waking consciousness) in its daily interface with our soul quality (higher Self). That interface happens through the functioning of our chakra system, which controls and influences the way we perceive reality through the four archetypes of what it is to be human (mental, physical, spiritual, emotional).

CHAKRA	NAME	CHARACTERISTIC	TO DO	TO LEARN
2	Sacral	Creationist	Create as a visionary	Create by acceptance and love of Self, allow to be loved
3	Solar Plexus	Charismatic Leader	Represent truth and power through individuation	Qualitative morals and ethics, individual power

CHAKRA	NAME	CHARACTERISTIC	TO DO	TO LEARN
4	Heart	Empath	To give, receive, and be love	To communicate emotionally
5	Throat	Communicator	Articulate meaning and comprehension, elucidation, illumination	Trust the feelings and intuition; to be grounded
6	Brow or Third Eye	Prophet	Inception of higher communication	To be in the heart center

What we incarnated to do in this lifetime is driven by our dominant chakra disposition, and even though it varies a little throughout life, we tend to stay within the orientation of that given dominant chakra for life.

However, the dominant chakra does color our disposition to perceive reality from a certain orientation, and thus helps predict the probable reactions based on how well the chakra dominant person is living in their higher aspect. The higher the aspect, the more self-actualized the person will be. The lower the chakra aspect, the more the person will be tossed about by the exigencies of their life experiences.

What we incarnated to learn in this lifetime is a function of the weakness of the dominant chakra, immersed in the illusion of separation and the fears and doubts of the linear mind. Fear and doubt will flee from the evolved mind.

For example, the 2 is in this lifetime to be the Creator and Visionary, but what he or she came to learn is self-acceptance. The 3 in this lifetime is here to experience personal power, and also how to learn to make emotional decisions regarding morals and ethics.

FEARS THAT DRIVE OUR WAKING CONSCIOUSNESS

Why do we behave the way we do? We are a *whole human being*, more than a set of learned behaviors.

We are multidimensional beings, simultaneously spirit and flesh, metaphysical and corporeal, and the way we make ourselves strong is to bring those two forces together: *Heaven on earth* (or, as above - so below, another Hermetic Principle).

How we make the effort to hold that balance defines the nature of our charactor in a given lifetime.

It is the interface between mind and spirit that presents such difficulty for us, because we've not yet found a way to directly measure, through our five senses, our metaphysical presence. But it exists as a part of us regardless.

Even as each chakra gifts us with its unique psychic ability, so also does that very power cause the ego to fear for itself.

It is this blending of the higher dimensional and third-dimensional reality that causes the suffering we encounter in life, for our physical minds assume that a temporal and spatial existence is all there is to reality.

Since our metaphysical reality is both in a higher dimension and a more eloquent expression of our soul, we can feel far removed from the awareness that we are *seamlessly integrated* with this higher level of existence. There is no difference between these two realms, except as we perceive there to be a difference, which is an illusion.

Thus the mind (linear and temporal) must capitulate to the stream of consciousness that flows from our soul presence through our chakras into our waking personalities. When the mind must deal with that higher level of knowing, it is just as difficult as trying to make a three-dimensional image leap off a piece of paper on which it was two-dimensionally drawn.

The physical mind cannot conceive of the higher dimensional reality of one's own consciousness, so in capitulation it creates fears from the illusion of separation.

CHAKRA	GREATEST FEARS	HARDEST THING YOU'LL EVER DO IN THIS LIFETIME
2	I cannot create anything greater than what came before. Nothing I do is enough.	*To accept and love your Self as much as anyone or anything.*
3	What could be true is true.	*To accept your power; that you are that powerful.*
4	That I am not pure. That my heart is not pure.	*To accept the purity you have earned from past lives, well-lived. To be love itself.*
5	No one knows me for who I truly am. Nothing I communicate or teach matters.	*To unite as above, so below: To unite Heaven and earth: To bring your spiritual nature into your corporeal presence.*
6	To never touch the earth plane. That life is a mental abstract.	*To unite universal mind, physical mind, and heart. To incept new paradigms.*

The following table illustrates the greatest fears of each chakra disposition.

When the mind capitulates to the strength of the given dominant chakra, it is trying to do in a linear and temporal manner that which is continuously happening in a higher level of consciousness. Since the mind cannot conceive of the totality of a higher level of awareness until the individual evolves to that state, the mind exerts its control through the greatest fear of that chakra level.

For instance, the greatest fear of 2's is they cannot create anything greater than that which came before. The second chakra is you (your consciousness) on a higher level. It is ever-unfolding, always creating and ever-evolving, no matter what your linear mind is thinking.

The mind, on some level, knows that it cannot conceive of the fullness of a state of being that exists, but is on a higher level than it can currently function. So the mind gets to control the possible outcomes by wishing for guarantees of a future outcome.

Some people respond to the power of their second chakra by becoming controlling, not desiring surprises, by becoming analytical, rigid and inflexible. Some respond in the other direction by spreading themselves too thin, trying to create with the mind what the second chakra creates ceaselessly, causing them to enter into chaos and uncertainty.

The measure of success in integrating the second chakra higher aspects into the personality is the amount of trust and faith through the *feelings* the person is willing to engender. The mind can think, but it is not enough to grasp the true multi-dimensional nature of who we are. And, the same lesson is true for any given chakra dominance.

It is by and through the feelings that the gap between mind and spirit, metaphysics and the physical realm is bridged. It is the ineffable, intangible true nature of our Selves that nonetheless exists, even if not directly palpable through the five senses. And since our metaphysical nature is no respecter of time or space, our higher expression of Self is available to us at all times, if we choose it.

Part of the trick in choosing is in the will to be vulnerable to your greatness. It is not a force of will that is outward (masculine energy). It is a force of will to *allow* (feminine energy) that will yield you to a higher expression of your Self. The ferocity with which you are willing to apply the Feminine Principle will determine your measure of success in bridging that gap.

As you cannot force your Self to understand, neither can you force your Self to be more evolved without the willingness to be open to a part of your experience that cannot yet be readily explained, but can be felt. This is not the type of feelings like joy or exuberance (though they can be a part of it). It is rather the essence of *beholding the experience,* as one beholds a mountain meadow of great beauty and purity. It is that higher part of your Self, unsullied by doubt or fear, the free land of limitless possibilities for the expression of your true nature.

The mind fears what it cannot know, but the heart yearns for what it feels is there nonetheless. It is the desire to pass beyond the fears of the mind with the open heart that yields to the epiphany of true spiritual growth; the kind that cannot be had through books or seminars, but by direct revelatory experience of being open and available to the Creator within.

REFERENCE CHAKRAS

All of our chakras work together in concert. However, this section is meant to depict a particularly strong association of the consciousness of one chakra that is referent to a major, dominant chakra. This "reference" creates the opportunity for a pattern of behavior where the perception-will-reaction is somewhat predictable, and so are the health consequences.

Do you remember our chakra number-naming convention? As an example, a 5-2 means "fifth chakra dominant with a reference to the second chakra." That is, the fifth chakra is the dominant influence in a person's life, affecting their disposition towards their mental, physical, spiritual, and emotional states of being. A reference to the second chakra means that the person will tend to have a secondary influence through the higher or lower aspects of the second chakra. For instance, if the person started to experience abundance issues, spread themselves too thin, or became chaotic, these are all characteristics of the lower aspect of the second chakra.

But if it is a reference, these issues usually show up if the dominant chakra (fifth, in this case) is first affected, or is in its own lower aspect (the person is ungrounded, is not communicating, etc.)

While we all have experiences related to all our chakras, there are some of us who have strong references chakras. And we may not experience a difficulty in those reference chakras until we are having a challenge in the dominant chakra first.

The dynamics of energy that occur are thus: If a person's dominant chakra is experiencing a difficulty or suffering, the chakra may siphon off energy from its most closely associated reference chakra. This is one of the reasons I tell students in my healer's training workshops to always look for the root cause of the problem, not necessarily what the client seems to be directly experiencing.

An example of a 5-2 in this circumstance would be if their lower back is experiencing pain that could normally be associated with the support and burden issues related to the second chakra. The problem could just as easily be mental, emotional, or spiritual. But on intuitive observation showing the person to be a 5-2, it could be that their fifth chakra is truly the dominant one and that they are suffering from being ungrounded, non-communicative, feeling separate, alone, detached, alienated and so forth. The lack of being grounded or suffering experienced through the fifth chakra initiated the troubles related to the second chakra. Without an intuitive experiential frame of reference it is easy to miss the true cause of a person's suffering, if they have a referent chakra relationship.

By applying energetic healing to the dominant chakra,

the problems in the second chakra can begin to clear by themselves. Healing depends on many factors, including the abilities of the healer, and any karma, mission statement or free-will choices on the part of the person being healed. (For an in-depth reading of reference chakras, please see The Book of Healing. It is a distillation of my 17-level Healer's Training Course of study in qualitative healing for the whole human being.)

In relationships, an individual can have reference chakras of their own, and be in relationship to another person who has a dominant chakra, but no reference. As you know, relationships exist on innumerable levels and vary greatly in their complexity and exchange of intimacy and energy. It is not the purpose of this book to define all relationships, but to give you an idea of how the energy exchange works between and among people, why we take the energetic relationships to people that we do, and how that exchange affects us on many levels.

Of the whole population that I have counseled for many years, at least one-third has referent chakras. Some of the most typical reference chakra relationships are described below.

COMMON REFERENCE CHAKRA RELATIONSHIPS

5-2

People who are throat-dominant often have the reference disposition of the second chakra (5-2), because the second chakra (known as the visceral chakra) provides the sensory visceral experience necessary to ground the fifth chakra person. The second chakra is very much the complement of the fifth, in that it provides a base of sensory experiences of the physical body that act as the living lightning rod to ground the powerful forces of articulation, and the healing of comprehension, found through the consciousness of the fifth chakra.

Our physical mind, in its capitulation through fear, subverts the truest expression of our Selves coming through the dominant chakra, and this is no less apparent in reference chakras.

Having a 5–2 relationship active, however, is like a built-in healing device, in that the qualities of the second chakra will help to heal the fifth. And the reverse is also true.

If a 5 is ungrounded, not communicating, or otherwise suffering through the fifth chakra, the energies that are depleted in the fifth chakra can be supplemented by taking them from the second chakra, thus creating problems there as well.

Any of the lower aspects of the second chakra can be displayed once the fifth chakra is affected.

2-5

The second chakra dominant person can have a strong relationship to their fifth chakra in order to help them articulate their passion/lustiness for life. The positive benefit is that there is a voice for the passion, vision, and multi-tasking capabilities of the 2.

The fifth chakra provides the means for articulation (communication in many forms) for the visceral nature of the second chakra. It is like the broadcasting station for the experiential rootedness of the second chakra; the means of sending out the possibility of communication of the great over-the-horizon view of the visionary.

The reverse is true here again, as it is for all reference chakras. If the 2 person is suffering in some way, he or she can exhibit the lack of grounding, physical pain, emotional unavailability, alienation, and any of the other problems related to the lower aspect of the second chakra.

Other common reference chakra relationships:
  2-3
  2-4
  3-4
  4-2

Less common reference chakra relationships:
  2-6
  6-2

It takes experience and trust to be able to recognize a person's dominant chakra, and referent chakra (if there is one). Understanding and applying the guidelines in this book can assist you. Certainly, there are as many combinations as there are possibilities, and you may see them in your own experience.

CHAPTER 4

DETERMINING YOUR DOMINANT CHAKRA

This chapter will help you to determine your dominant chakra, and anyone else's you care to assess. Please note a few suggestions:

- This is not meant to be entirely conclusive: we are evolving beings, constantly changing and making free-will choices.

- Do not cubbyhole your Self into a given dominant chakra. All our chakras are working seamlessly, and thus have intertwining effects though our consciousness.

- We all have our challenges in the consciousness of each chakra. Even though dominant in one, there is always some illusion that compels us to create lessons for the benefit of our life's experiences. The seeds of karma are stored in each chakra, and as long as we have chakras, we have some karma.

- This chapter is a tool to assist you in developing a better sense of how the higher part of your Self, your metaphysical nature, helps guide your life through a given dominant chakra. Pay attention to the strengths and weaknesses of each chakra and see where you feel (not think) you fit.

- Take your assessment and share it with a trusted friend and see what their reaction is. That is, see if they observe you in the same way. Of course, if you really want to make this interesting, do the assessment on them first before you speak with them. Listen to their responses and see if they behave in a manner that is consistent with the dominant chakra disposition you determined for them.

- Read Eye of the Lotus for a more in-depth look at each chakra type, especially the chapter on how to prevent psychic manipulation. You may find something there to help you identify your dominant chakra.

- Read the Case Histories section at the end of this book. They will give you great insight into the lives and relationships of different dominant chakra individuals.

- Go into prayer and meditation, and ask for the inner guidance to see your Self clearly. Practicing these techniques will result in more accurate assessments, but they work best if you trust your feelings first, then think.

GET OUT OF YOUR HEAD

The first thing to do is to get out of your head and into your heart. Not into the sentimental heart, but the heart of feelings and intuition; your higher sense perceptions. This assessment will work best if you are authentic about your Self and willing to own up to your tendencies and habituations. Granted, you won't have all the insights, but the effort of doing this work is what is helping to define you. Don't worry about the goal, just make the effort.

OK, here we go; you'll be choosing the best (and worst) attributes from each chakra, and you'll end up with the most marks in the chakra that appears to be your dominant one. You'll probably see many parts of your Self in the different chakras. This is normal.

The following table shows the average spread/distribution of chakra dominance that I've observed among the population I've counseled for more than twenty years.

DOMINANT CHAKRA	ASPECT	PERCENT OF THE TOTAL POPULATION
2 Sacral	Creationist	40%
3 Solar Plexus	Charismatic Leader	28%
4 Heart	Empath	4%
5 Throat	Communicator	28%
6 Brow	Prophet	.002%

GRAB A PENCIL

Start checking off traits that apply to you on the lists that follow. Count the number of check marks for each chakra. Note that there are many more items for the second chakra than any other. This does not mean that everyone is second chakra dominant; it just means we all have far more things going on in the second chakra than any other because it is the most visceral.

Look at the total check marks, but also see which attributes are the most pertinent to you.

SECOND CHAKRA (SACRAL) STRENGTHS, WEAKNESSES, AND HOW TO HEAL

SECOND CHAKRA: STRENGTHS

- ❏ Creationist - one who can create a solution or an alternative when there seems to be none - when no one else can provide an option, you just come up with one
- ❏ One who can see the potential in others
- ❏ Visionary - one who "sees over the curve of the earth" or can psychically tell what is coming
- ❏ Energy of the Mystic - can accurately see others as how they could be "whole and complete"
- ❏ One who sees the big picture - the larger overall view for a project or the direction of family dynamics or the future of events unfolding
- ❏ One who sees infinite alternatives
- ❏ Pioneer - one who blazes the trail when no one else would or will - some examples in history are individuals who endeavored to make inventions or advanced human development when no one else would believe such things were possible
- ❏ Explorer - one who does not have a path, but forges ahead based on faith - explorers do not have paths, otherwise it would not be exploring
- ❏ The Labyrinth, the Walk of Faith

❏ The Fierce Lover
❏ Show-er of human potential
❏ Life of faith and trust
❏ Risk-taker
❏ People pleaser
❏ Master of many trades, jack of none
❏ Apocalyptic
❏ Way-shower
❏ Harmonizer
❏ Catalyst - things happen when you show up
❏ Analytical - why they put the word "anal" in analysis
❏ Healer
❏ One who inspires others
❏ Bringer of the new way of doing things
❏ Sensuality, the Lusty Human Being
❏ Hedonist
❏ Sexuality
❏ Sensuous (of the senses deeply rooted)
❏ Passionate about life
❏ The Warrior

SECOND CHAKRA: WEAKNESSES OR CHALLENGES

❏ One who can suddenly change
❏ Loss of identity
❏ Loss of integrity
❏ Loss of inspiration
❏ No matter what you do, it is never good enough
❏ Losing everything, then starting over with nothing
❏ Clinical depression
❏ The Victim

- ❏ The Martyr
- ❏ Abundance issues (mental, physical, spiritual, emotional)
- ❏ Abuse issues
- ❏ Abandonment issues
- ❏ Self-destruction, self-loathing
- ❏ Chaotic or attracts chaos often
- ❏ Reverse-manipulator
- ❏ Manipulates others through chaos
- ❏ Faithlessness
- ❏ Hopelessness
- ❏ The Energy Vampire or needy personality
- ❏ Vindictiveness
- ❏ Dispersing or squandering one's resources
- ❏ Controlling behavior
- ❏ False humility, self-effacing
- ❏ Passive-aggressive
- ❏ Remorse, regret, guilt
- ❏ Resentment
- ❏ The Recovering Perfectionist – compelled to do everything perfectly, but cannot
- ❏ Rejected by others when trying to help them
- ❏ Spread too thin with multiple priorities/obligations
- ❏ Co-dependent enabler

TO HEAL THE SECOND CHAKRA

- Perspective through inspiration
- Freedom to create
- Healthy emotional boundaries

- The perception of infinite alternatives
- Alone time, time for your Self
- A fierce love of your Self
- Reduce the number of multiple, simultaneous obligations.
- Don't try to fix everyone
- Don't assume responsibilities for which you are not responsible
- Allow your Self to receive love
- Receive as much as you give
- Live a life of faith and trust
- Live your passion
- Allow your Self to be the true mystic; correctly, intuitively, perceiving others
- Hold the vision, the big picture, without getting bogged down in details
- Accept your Self as good enough
- Cherish your Self - do nothing to denigrate your character.

THIRD CHAKRA (SOLAR PLEXUS) STRENGTHS, WEAKNESSES, AND HOW TO HEAL

THIRD CHAKRA: STRENGTHS

- ❏ Bearer of truth
- ❏ Alone against the crowd in your own authenticity
- ❏ Virtuous holder of the unique power of inner truth
- ❏ Helps others to individuate their personal strengths and truth by your example.
- ❏ The ability to be "right" - sometimes doing the right thing is not the logical thing
- ❏ Charismatic leader - one who knows the way of virtue
- ❏ Moral and ethical character - choosing to make the difficult choice that offers harmony at the expense of ignorance of others
- ❏ Hierophant (spiritual seeker) - one who quests for the truth in various teachings, teachers, and chooses the higher teachings to live by
- ❏ The Manipulator - neither good nor bad, must decide how to use power
- ❏ Incisiveness - able to get to the "bottom line" with your intuition
- ❏ Spiritual but not religious - has an inner connection to the truth that will transcend all religious and dogmatic teachings - goes from belief to knowing

❏ Truth as a virtue: Are you the only one in the room who's "right"? Sometimes, yes – and you hold to it no matter what

❏ Spiritual leader – doesn't have to be your occupation, but rather holding a state of being or awareness of higher truth in consciousness

❏ Defender of those who cannot defend themselves – stands up for the "little guy" or for those who are innocent

❏ Innocent – no caveat, no hidden agenda, no ulterior motive

❏ Protector of the innocent – people who are innocent tend to seek you out

❏ Counselor – people ask your advice as to what is the "right" thing to do

❏ The True Skeptic – the healthy skeptic who asks the questions that must be asked

❏ The Manifestor – you can make things happen, make material things (money, belongings, etc.) manifest

❏ Harmony vs. conflict – able to use moral and ethical values to perceive the emotional choice between the pairs of opposites

❏ Show others how to individuate their power by your example of standing for what you believe in

❏ Person of ultimates – one willing to make the choice to act, when the outcome is unknown

❏ Righteous anger at the iniquities of the world – your anger is just and reasoned, and used only to motivate change

THIRD CHAKRA: WEAKNESSES OR CHALLENGES

❑ Power struggles

❑ Manipulator for personal gain

❑ Procrastinator against decisions or actions

❑ Hidden anger or holding anger

❑ The need to be right

❑ Loss of identity, comparison to others

❑ Self-worth, self-esteem, confidence issues

❑ Hungry for power, education, money, etc., at the expense of wisdom

❑ Takes things personally

❑ The Narcissist; vanity issues

❑ Confused when making emotional decisions

❑ The need to be right whether you're right or not

TO HEAL THE THIRD CHAKRA

• Stimulate acknowledgement of your Self

• Accept that truth is universal, your truth is unique to you

• Seek higher spiritual authority

• Accept yourself as powerful; yield to your inner power

• Allow your Self to experience power

• Emphasize that which is unique about you

• Stay in your power

• Stay in your truth

• Do not procrastinate

• Accept your innocence, no caveat

• Do not give away your power to attain peace

FOURTH CHAKRA (HEART)
STRENGTHS, WEAKNESSES, AND HOW TO HEAL

FOURTH CHAKRA: STRENGTHS

- ❏ The Empath - one who deeply feels what others feel, even before they feel it
- ❏ One who represents the quality of what loving compassion is
- ❏ Pureness in heart - your heart really is that pure
- ❏ The Healer - people feel that you never run out of energy, that they can tap into your healing heart anytime
- ❏ The Conserver and Preserver - one who represents the conservation of purity in the world as that purity externalizes in many forms, from ecology to museums to health (mental, spiritual, emotional, physical)
- ❏ Emotional anchor with healthy boundaries - you successfully anchor huge groups of people as the emotional empathy
- ❏ Person of symmetry (puts others into symmetry) - often externalizes in choice of avocations, like architecture, engineering, mathematics, music, sculpture, etc.
- ❏ Embodies the Feminine Principle - the power of the will to allow in, instead of to push out

❏ Relationship with Fairy Kingdom, a subset of the Deva kingdom, which includes nature spirits

❏ Relationship with nature spirits - wind, lakes, water, mountains, etc.

❏ The many-spoked wheel, who, as an empath, psychically anchors an entire group of people

FOURTH CHAKRA: WEAKNESSES OR CHALLENGES

❏ Human emotional pincushion

❏ Suffers quietly

❏ Emotional despot

❏ False humility, hiding one's power

❏ Withholding love

❏ Gullible and naïve

❏ Poor emotional communicator

❏ The Emotional Saboteur

❏ Loss of identity

TO HEAL THE FOURTH CHAKRA

• Stay emotionally grounded

• Accept your Self as pure

• Water release technique (exercise from <u>Eye of the Lotus</u>)

• Healthy emotional boundaries

• Love your Self as much as anyone or anything

• Never sabotage your feelings

• Being naïve is OK in innocence, but use discernment in relationships

• Accept the purity you represent that you've earned through past life dharma

- It's OK for others to heal, just because you exist
- Do what you love and place a value on it
- Allow your Self to be emotionally correct when empathically observing others
- Do not take on suffering so that others may heal - transmute instantly any negativity you take on
- Communicate as well as you can, knowing no human tongue can express its fullness, and no human ear can hear its purity

FIFTH CHAKRA (THROAT)
STRENGTHS, WEAKNESSES, AND HOW TO HEAL

FIFTH CHAKRA: STRENGTHS

❏ The Teacher - one who represents teachings or higher level of understanding to others - never has to mean "teacher" in the strict sense, but rather the teachings that can be discerned through one's actions

❏ The Communicator - can have many forms - voice, music, math, email, etc.

❏ Comprehension - one who heals the mind of others to gain a higher level of comprehension

❏ Living nexus point of energy, facilitator for movement - people can sometimes cycle quickly into and out of your life, having completed their karmic relationship

❏ The Expediter - your presence seems to make things happen

❏ Articulator of communication - a deeper understanding of the real message, leading from understanding to true comprehension

❏ Healer of meaning - your presence, through the 5th chakra, heals others ability to attain true meaning, as well as your own

❏ Healer of comprehension - your presence or awareness heals the mind of another to gain a greater comprethension of an idea, thought, concept – helps the other to go from concept to awareness

❑ Healer of understanding – your presence, through the 95% that is energy, increases the possibility that true understanding can take place

❑ Bringer of Heaven on earth – all chakra types do this, but here it means to bring the spirit and the body together in balance

❑ The Ambassador – one who paves the way and can use tact and decorum or diplomacy to assuage a situation

❑ The Coordinator – able to connect the right people and events together

❑ The Networker – similar to the coordinator, you are able to increase the level of communication and connection with people and events

FIFTH CHAKRA: WEAKNESSES OR CHALLENGES

❑ False Prophet (#1) – giving misleading information or explanations

❑ The Mentalist – living within mental abstracstions, distancing your Self from emotional reality

❑ The Know it All – a defense that is fear-based where you pretend to know a little about everything so as not to be perceived as not "with it"

❑ The Emotional Hermit – the desire to deal with humanity/problems by distancing yourself as much as possible from others

❑ The Emotionally Distant Individual – carrying on relationships (intimate, familial, parental, etc.) without really being emotionally involved – saying all the right words but being emotionally detached so as to avoid emotional overwhelm from being too grounded

❏ Detached from reality
❏ Aloof
❏ Floating through life like a helium balloon on a string
❏ Alone in a crowd
❏ Life is not efficacious or productive - the sense that you are not achieving in this life what you had set out to do, or that what you do has little relevance or meaning

TO HEAL THE FIFTH CHAKRA

- Stay grounded and in your body as much as you can

- Trust your feelings, not just whether you have them but whether you are trusting them

- Do not mentalize

- Stay present in the moment

- Improve your patience

- Make eye contact with others, and feel your physical presence

- Breathe mindfully and deeply - feel the soles of your feet on the ground

- Engage in a regulated breathing practice, like yoga , Tai Chi, or Chi Gong

- Be careful what you think you have to know - watch what you put into your mind - watch out for the glamour of too complete an understanding

- Hug and embrace in your relationships - make physical contact

SIXTH CHAKRA (THIRD EYE) STRENGTHS, WEAKNESSES, AND HOW TO HEAL

SIXTH CHAKRA: STRENGTHS

❑ The Prophet - one who holds the vision of the future in our highest potential as realized beings

❑ Bringer of the New Paradigm - a state of being that incepts the paradigm that has not before existed

❑ The Clairsentient - knows what "cannot be known" - one of the most evolved psychic abilities

❑ The Person Out of Time - one who is not limited to the common thinking and belief systems of the current age

SIXTH CHAKRA: WEAKNESSES OR CHALLENGES

❑ False Prophet (#2) - engaging in lower astral relationships, revealing information that is misleading or very egocentric

❑ The Autist

❑ The Abstract Mentalist - one who goes way too far into abstraction

❑ Emotional imbalance - one who has difficulty taking an emotion from a thought form into a feeling

❑ Multiple Personality Disorder - engaging more than one personality at a time emanating into this dimension

TO HEAL THE SIXTH CHAKRA

- Center in the heart
- Be with people who want nothing from you, who are tender with you
- Cherish your mind as brilliant, yet fragile – use your fragility as a strength, not a weakness
- Be gentle with your Self
- Never underestimate your gifts of clairsentience
- It is OK to be who you are

CHAPTER 5

THE LAW OF RECIPROCITY:
HOW WE TAKE ENERGETIC
RELATIONSHIPS TO EACH OTHER
(LIKE ATTRACTS UNLIKE)

This chapter is the key to the whole book. Understand the Law of Reciprocity and you will have much greater insight into why you attract the relationships into your life the way you do, and how the dynamics of the energy (consciousness) in these relationships works between you.

You may remember reciprocals from school: the reciprocal of 2/3 is 3/2, or the multiplicative inverse of 7 is 1/7. In the language of energetic relationships it is how we take an *inverse* relationship to each other's skill sets.

That is, we tend to attract to us those people who represent the inverse of our skills, emotional wants, and needs. We invite relationships into our lives that help us to build on the lower aspects of our given dominant chakras, and relationships that help us to strengthen our weaknesses. Those people represent the consciousness that is the fulfillment of our perceived (and unconscious) weaknesses.

For instance, a 5 might have a relationship to a 2, so that the 5 will help the 2 to articulate what they cannot say, and the

2 will help the 5 to see the bigger picture or to feel more of their sensual (grounded, or of the five senses) nature.

One important point to remember is that we are ceaselessly sending out the *qualitative emanations* of our true selves, our dominant chakras, in all directions at all times in infinite combinations. It does not matter if you are in an elevator, a restaurant, or movie theater. You are sending out the quality of who you are to all around you, and you are also receiving the psychic energy from those around you, as well. We take a psychic relationship to each other long before the mind ever thinks a single thought.

So, we will attract those people to us who help fulfill our soul's purpose no matter where we go or what we do. Life is a matter of developing one's character through the responses (free will) to the circumstances and people we attract.

Remember, we send out the energy of who we really are and what we represent at all times, no matter what our minds are thinking or doing. You are constantly engaging in energetic relationships with others, and you will psychically take a relationship to each other, long before the mind catches on and starts to think.

Our consciousness is ceaselessly setting the script in advance for certain people, certain jobs, relationships, and events to enter our lives. Do not assume that we are pre-destined, that there really are no choices. It is better to think of your Self as an actor on the stage; you have your script, costume, fellow actors, props, and stage. But how you read your lines is up to you. Your fellow actors will respond in their scripts more fully in the play the better you read your lines. Act after act, life unfolds in a pageantry of choices, made more significant by the choice to live in the possibility of synchronicity.

Your fellow actors have their scripts and the free will to choose how they will act, and even if it may seem that you can exert influence, the only script you truly have control over is your own. Understanding this chapter and the case histories will show you how the dynamics of these scripts create the possibility to change and to enhance the interaction in your relationships.

Those people we attract and interact with can include karma from past lives, a mission statement for this life, and pure free will, but we incarnate into soul groups for the purpose of our mutual evolution.

In other words, we are not just doing this by ourselves, but working together in an energetic collaborative leadership (a Oneness) where we are not separate from each other, but the perception that we are causes us to engage in those energetic relationships.

We are mutual actors in the same play, and it unfolds every moment in our lives in that pageantry of successive events. It is always wise to remember that you really are in charge of your life, and that you really do have choices.

Reciprocity is the yin and yang, up and down, complementary forces that when brought together form the union of the two. That union represents strength and wholeness - it is why we seek partners, family, love, sex, money, and more. But, it is a union, a joining of two forces that are working together.

Your strength is your weakness and your weakness is your strength.

When you lift weights and feel resistance in your muscles, what eventually happens? Your muscle fibers tear down and then build up stronger. This process/principle is also true in the metaphysics of our lives. Our weakness is our strength. That is, if we keep working on that which makes us weak, we build the spiritual muscles, awaken the higher-sense-perceptions, become strong and see things as they truly are, not as they seem to be.

We suffer because we live in the illusion of being separate from what we seek. It's a really, really good illusion, but an illusion nonetheless.

The Law of Reciprocity guarantees that we will bring to us relationships that work on our weaknesses (imbalance and illusion) in order to make us strong spiritually. Remember, all healing boils down to only one thing – overcoming any illusion that separates us from the Oneness in which we already live.

So, in effect, everyone is a healer who can bring about change in the world by living their life well, by working out in the "chakra gym" of life's challenges.

If you are alive, you are already in relationships that are designed to help you strengthen your character, even if it doesn't seem that way.

Always in metaphysics there is a hidden part or benefit to the actions we undertake. In the case of the yin and yang, two forces that come together form the third force, which is the union between the two. The hidden, or fourth force, is that all unity still implies separation (two things together are still two things) and that all unity will eventually head towards *fusion.*

Fusion is the absorption of the union into homogeneity, where there is no difference between one part and another. As on the higher levels we are androgynous (both sexes together), so also are we truly in a Oneness where there is no separation, not even through the suggestion of union.

As we engage others for the development of our soul's purpose in what we came to do and to learn, we reflect back to ourselves the qualities that are externalizations of our soul's desires.

The level and intensity of the reciprocity will, of course, change between dominant chakra personalities from, say, a social setting to an intimate encounter. You'll see many examples of this in the Case Histories section.

One chakra dominance is not better than another – just another form of experience meant to develop the nature of our character in the evolution of our soul quality. Please don't get the idea that if someone is fourth chakra (heart) dominant, that his or her life path is any more important or sacred than yours.

There are different levels of evolvement, but no one's path is more important than anyone else's. If you live in Oneness, how could it be so? If you think the Dalai Lama's path is more important than yours, then that is your *illusion.*

CHAPTER 6

THE LAW OF REPRESENTATION THROUGH RELATIONSHIP
(LIKE ATTRACTS LIKE)

Thought you had it all figured out? This chapter is important too! Just as we attract people into our lives that represent the inverse of our strengths or skill-sets, we also create relationships to build on positive attributes.

Representation Through Relationship sounds like a mouthful, but it is fairly simple. For example, when Mark Victor Hansen and Jack Canfield, authors of <u>Chicken Soup for the Soul</u> and many other books, decided they needed to start making over 100 million dollars a year to help more people through philanthropy, what did they do?

Well, they started hanging out with people who made over 100 million dollars a year. Since most of our communication is energy, the idea of "like attracts like" is not so difficult to understand. By hanging out with those individuals who represent the highest ideals (especially those who are evolved spiritually) we tend to become "overshadowed" by the qualities they possess.

Look at the disciples who hung out with Jesus, the monks who studied with the Buddha, people who follow the teachings of the Dalai Lama, and you get my point. You are actually taking a psychic relationship to what they represent.

Spend a lot of time with an enlightened being and what do you think happens? Especially if you embrace the 95% of subtle energy of our awareness, connecting deeply with the other?

So we affiliate or associate ourselves with those qualities we wish to imbue ourselves. By the conscious choice to make that affiliation, we open ourselves up to be influenced by the positive attributes we seek.

It is the will to open or allow (the Feminine Principle) that yields us to the possibility of a greater consciousness. It is not merely a process of mental focus, but rather surrendering to our limitlessness.

Intuitively, the more we trust our feelings in associations with individuals who hold the ideals and awareness to which we aspire, the more we open to grow into the consciousness of what Sogyal Rinpoche (author of The Tibetan Book of Living and Dying) calls our "true selves."

Recall the saying: "If you ever want to know how your life is going, look around and see who your friends are." Remember, karma is basically the law of cause and effect and reflects the Chinese axiom: "If you don't change the road you're on, you're bound to end up where you're headed!"

The truth in this is that at any time, you have a *choice*. You can choose to continue old patterns or change by relating yourself with those people or teachings that represent a higher level of consciousness.

Even when you read a book, listen to a speech, look at a painting or movie, you are also tuning in to the consciousness of the originator. Next time you buy a book and really resonate with it, you are attracted to the like qualities of the author. People who read books by inspired and evolved authors are taking a psychic relationship to what those authors represent.

Take a look at where you are in life right now. Look at your family, friends, and associations, what you read, what you spend time on, and what you believe.

If you wish to improve your life, look at what qualities you are relating to, and decide if they represent the qualities to which you aspire.

It is by effort that we grow. Don't worry that it may take a day, a year, or a lifetime. It is the effort that defines you.

CHAPTER 7

TYPICAL CHAKRA-
TYPE RELATIONSHIPS

There are many human relationships that occur on many levels - friends, rivals, intimates, ex's, relatives, co-workers, etc. This chapter discusses the opportunity of growth, from both harmony and conflict, when specific chakra types get together.

You will first read of even/odd (e.g., 2-5) chakra pairs in relationships, along with examples of the more common pairings.

Later, we'll look at even/even, and odd/odd pairs of chakras (e.g., 2-4 and 5-3).

And finally, we'll cover examples of same-chakra type (e.g., 2-2) relationships.

As a note of interest from my book, <u>Eye of the Lotus: Psychology of the Chakras,</u> women's odd-numbered chakras (1, 3, 5, 7) spin counterclockwise, and their even-numbered chakras (2, 4, 6) spin clockwise.

For men, it is just the opposite. Men's odd-numbered chakras (1, 3, 5, 7) spin clockwise, and their even-numbered chakras (2, 4, 6) spin counterclockwise.

But this is not a hard-and-fast rule, and there really is no "spin" physically. I've seen many variations in the thousands of people I've counseled over the years, but it does give rise to the thought of how the coupling and flow of energies and their dynamics play out in relationships.

Remember, we bring all forms of relationships into our lives as reflections of ourselves, ultimately to heal the illusion of separation.

EVEN AND ODD-NUMBERED DOMINANT CHAKRAS: *WHAT HAPPENS WHEN THEY GET TOGETHER*

Even-odd chakra pairs come in many flavors, 5-2, 3-4, 2-5 and so on. You can see the possibilities: chakra types 2, 3, 4, 5, 6 in all their various combinations. But it seems the most popular relationships are 2-5, 3-4 and 2-3, which I will detail in this chapter in their generalities.

The even-odd pairing seems to be much more prevalent than the same chakra (e.g., 2-2, 5-5, etc.) pairings. One other point: since there are very few sixth chakra people you won't see very many relationships involving them, but there are some.

People dominant in the same chakra have infinite variations influenced by mission statement, karma, and free will. That means that a given chakra-dominant person could attract many variations of another chakra-dominant personality into their life to present many variations on a theme, until they overcome the lesson and/or karma associated with the relationship.

Here are a couple of even-odd relationships:

5-2 RELATIONSHIP

Let's start with a 5-2 relationship. I find this type very common and the balancing act is pretty easy to follow. The fifth chakra person is the articulator of information and comprehension but lacks grounding and must come to trust their feelings, not just the strength of their mentality. The second chakra person is the passionate, sensory and sensuous visionary, but lacks the self-acceptance, validation, and personal faith to see their own beingness and future clearly.

When this pair gets together, what is the balance? The 2 incarnates to be the visionary or creationist, but they come to learn self-acceptance and that what they do is good enough. Typically, the 5 will help the 2 to see themselves clearly and to help give meaning to their visions.

The 2's sometimes suffer from having great visions, but cannot always get them going and growing. Part of the problem of being a visionary is that you can be born ahead of your time. Though there are some who will argue the point, I put forth in Eye of the Lotus, regarding "Dominant Chakra Types Throughout History," that Jesus was a very second chakra person as he was certainly ahead of his time. He pointed to a possibility for all humankind that was attainable through faith and trust.

A 5 will help to increase the comprehension of a 2's vision for themselves, increase the ability for the 2 to articulate that vision into a concrete reality, and help provide a framework for the meaning of 2's passion for life. Think of a 2 as the flowers in your backyard. If all you ever do is water and feed them, what happens? You have a chaotic jungle. 2's require the discipline of healthy emotional boundaries, but also to reduce the grandiosity of the vision to an attainable reality.

Sounds like a contradiction, that you're lessening the vibrancy and vitality of the vision. But it means that 2's typically have too many irons in the fire, and suffer from having too many multiple shared priorities.

Enter the balance of the fifth chakra mindfulness. While 5's are usually too much in their minds (hence why they may attract a 2), they can also balance the 2 by the same practical, pragmatic, and rational capabilities of a physical mind.

Sometimes, when 2's are overwhelmed by their own visionary capabilities, they become too analytical, which is a fear-based response the mind engages to cope with the grandeur of the vision of the 2. The 5 can help the passionate wildflower of the 2 stay focused on the vision, even if the 5 cannot understand the vision itself. The 95% of communication that is non-verbal, especially if the 5 is grounded, is what helps the 2 to stay on track, have faith, validate that what they do is good enough, and avoid spreading themselves too thinly.

What reflection does a 2 provide to a 5? The 5 incarnates as the teacher, the communicator, the emissary of understanding in a world habituated in a lower level of understanding. You can hear 5's say, "Am I the only one in the room who knows what's going on?" Often, yes. But what the 5 comes to learn is to trust their feelings. Not whether they have feelings, but to trust the feelings they have.

The mind capitulates, as it does with any chakra dominance, in a fear-based relationship of trying to control their perceptions/will/reactions to the third-dimensional environment. The mind, on its own, is incapable of doing this, of comprehending a larger version of itself. The mind, in its separation, tends to think it is complete in itself. But it can be done through the transcendence of the feeling-state.

This is where the 2 comes in: the most visceral of all chakras, the most connected to the five senses, and yet the one requiring the most faith in one's own inner vision. Many times, people who surround the 2 often just love to give the 2 their opinion of how the 2 should live. Partly this is because others are tuning into the 2's infinite capability and capacity to create something from nothing, which is the blessing and the curse.

The blessing is that the second chakra is ever unfolding, self evolving, and always creating, no matter what the mind is thinking. The curse (not really a curse, but a challenge) is that the 2 must learn to also create for themselves a part of the beneficence they create for the world around them. Good intentions alone are not enough: 2's must learn to allow themselves to receive as much as they create. If the 2 learns this lesson, there is so much more to offer the 5.

The 2 grounds the 5 in the visceral, feeling, passion, and rich mud of humanity and life. The 2 offers subtle and not-so-subtle alternatives to the 5's "too much in their mind" attitude toward life, through the 2's vision and passionate/sensual nature. The 2 helps the 5 to feel, though not all feelings are pleasant and attractive. And by feeling, the 5 may come to trust those feelings, as the 2 must through their lessons in faith.

The 2 is the antidote to the 5's escape to the mind without trust in the feelings, while the 5 is the antidote to the 2's escape to the feelings, without the practicality of mind.

The better a given chakra dominant person does in their own life, the more they have to offer everyone whom they encounter, and the reflections (reciprocities) have the possibility of becoming more holistic, profound, and life-changing. I say possibility because we all have a free-will choice how to react. Any of us can bring a master teacher into our lives. What we do with those teachings is up to us.

Remember, a second chakra person could attract any manner of chakra types into their lives as a reflection of the externalization of their search for balance, and the fifth chakra person can do precisely the same. If you understand that your higher nature has been and always is performing this balancing act (whether your conscious mind is aware of it or not), then it helps you to become more empowered in your decisions for your Self and your relationships, on all levels.

3-4 RELATIONSHIP

A third chakra personality is usually based on three criteria; what I call the three-legged stool. That is, their life is about power, uniqueness, and truth. Take away one leg of the stool and it will fall over. 3's are truth-givers and truth seekers; they tend to look for the truth as the bottom line, the essence of something, or as Western philosophers would say, "the thing itself." This manifests in many ways through the consciousness of the 3: the skeptic, the scientist, the protector of the innocent, the student of life, the seeker of truth, and so on.

The 3 comes to give truth to the world, to help others individuate their uniqueness and personal power, and to seek levels of spirituality that are beyond religion and dogma. The truth will transcend all religious and dogmatic attempts to frame it. What the 3 comes to learn is to make emotional (qualitative) decisions, based on the relevance of their own (individuated) truth. They must decide what is uniquely true for them in the feeling state, not just the mechanical or perfunctory state of common affairs.

The 3 comes to learn to accept that they are indeed powerful, that they incarnated in this lifetime to accept that power, and to experience personal power and truth in their uniqueness.

The fourth chakra personality incarnates to experience and to represent the quality of what love is. They've usually had a couple of sequential past lives of dharma (right action, right behavior), in which they accomplished what they came to do. The living of lives well accumulates individual merit. The merit allows them to reincarnate through the law of grace (some of their karma is relieved without having to pay it off) into this lifetime as heart chakra (4) dominant, with much purity of heart. But one of the hardest things a 4 will do is to accept the purity they've earned from past lives lived well.

The key is the word "earned." Their purity is not a gift, but an achievement of personal merit that they now must experience in this lifetime.

The qualitative emanations of the 4 are healing itself. Many people, though unconsciously, are drawn to the 4 as a healer. So everyone wants a little psychic piece of the 4, assuming the purity within the 4 will heal them. By now you know that this is really a reflection or reciprocity. The 4 person does not heal them, but represents the quality of healing and love. People who take a psychic relationship to this quality begin to heal because it awakens in them their own higher sense-perceptions that their legacy, too, is in the Oneness, beyond separation.

All the students in my Healer's Training Course are taught this fundamental philosophy of what true healing is. The healer does no healing, but rather represents the quality of healing itself by allowing all the vastness of the total consciousness God to flow through them.

The 4 comes to be the quality of what love is, and many times has difficulty knowing what to do. I tell them to do what they love, and to put a value on it. Placing a value on themselves forces the 4 to make a commitment to the perfection that already exists within them. Like the second chakra person, they must love themselves as much as they love others, and they must allow themselves to be loved as much as they love others.

The 4 comes to learn to communicate emotionally. If they represent love, how hard could that be? Because the profundity of love that comes through the heart chakra is from a higher level, no human being can fully communicate that quality in this dimension, though many have evoked us to that higher level though art, music, poetry, etc. Remember, what a person comes to learn is not the accomplishment, but the effort.

What happens when a 3 and 4 reflect qualities back to each other? There can be many variations, but following are some of the main points.

The 3 reflects back to the 4 the individuation of their power, even if it is in contention or done bluntly. The 3 helps the 4 to exhibit healthy emotional boundaries because usually the 4 is quite the empath (a person who psychically feels everything another person *feels*, even to the extent of taking on the negative compressive energy from that other person).

What happens if the 4 meets a 3 who desires to take nothing from them? Or what happens if the 4 meets a 3 who is a terrible manipulator of others? By definition 3's are manipulators who have to decide how they're going to experience the use of their power.

Some 4's will have a relationship with a 3 that has much suffering. The 3 needs to be right no matter what. The 4 is the peace-maker, the harmonizer but has not yet developed enough healthy emotional boundaries, therefore the 4 becomes the human emotional pincushion, taking on all the pain and suffering of the one-sided relationship.

Why invite this reflection to the 4? So the 4 can individuate their power, even though this is a painful lesson. One could say, "What did that 4 do, to attract such a relationship?" Have you ever heard of toxic relationships, addictive behaviors, the abused-wife syndrome? The energetic mechanics of such relationships play out the reflections in many ways, until the lesson is learned, and sometimes, the lesson is not learned fully.

As one of my teachers would say: "Perhaps we'll see them in the next lifetime."

Could the 4 learn the same lesson if the 3 were the beneficent dictator? That is, if the 3 were a powerful, but loving personality? Perhaps, but lessons are taught in all manner of expression, and this dimension is often the author of pain as an effective teaching tool to show how the illusion of separation causes suffering.

As difficult as it may be to read, there is indeed an eloquent expression of the creative aspect of the universe (God), as teacher, to co-create with us in a collaborative leadership the events and circumstances that will unfold before us to assist in the most effective and loving manner the emancipation of our consciousness from the shackles of illusion.

The 3 reflects to the 4 the possibility of "what could be true, is true." That is, the 3 must learn to accept that they really are that powerful, and they will emanate this quality to the 4 by virtue of their relationship through the 95% of communication that is energy.

So, the 4 has the opportunity to learn what personal power is, the concept of personal power, of not giving your power away in order to make other people happy, of the need *not* to be the harmonizer, of the possibility to allow others (with true compassion) to suffer, if they must, if that is their choice, so they can fully learn their life's lessons.

The 3 reflects to the 4 that the 4 can receive as much love as they give; that there is value in regarding the personality as valuable and viable. Here, we may seem to have a contradiction in two ways. First, Buddhists will tell you: "You must empty your cup before you can fill it," meaning, you spend your whole life learning who you are so that in the end you can let it all go! Second, saints and sages have told us that we must love unconditionally and give of ourselves freely like Mother Teresa working among the poor and infirm in Calcutta.

But central to both points is that *unless you first allow your Self to receive love and accept your Self as a part of God you cannot be effectively whole and complete* (if you care for others, but not your Self; if you love others, but do not accept love; if you heal others, but do not heal your Self). So, the 3 can help reflect back to the 4 the wisdom of the Self, in that nurturing your Self is the same as nurturing others.

A swami once said: "When I don't know who I am, I serve you. When I do know who I am, I am you."

So, what would the 4 reflect back to the 3? What is the reciprocity? The quality of the 4 is love itself with no caveat and no hidden agenda. The more noble 3's have no hidden agendas, caveats, or ulterior motives. They are what's called "plain vanilla," or what you see is what you get. The 4 represents love itself, the most perfect symmetry that can exist. The 4 represents "unconditionality" where no justification for itself is necessary. The 4 can represent a place or setting of repose for the powerful 3, a place for the tiger to eventually become the dragon.

That is, the tiger is smart and quick, but does not have the evolved sense of wisdom and realization of the dragon. The tiger is quick to react; the dragon awaits the perfect moment. The tiger thinks, the dragon knows. All tigers eventually become dragons. The 4 helps the 3 become a more eloquent expression of themselves, allows them the space to be at ease with their own power, and the 4 represents no contention or power struggle to the 3. If there is, then the 4 would be in their lower aspect as a victim, pincushion, emotional hostage, etc., working in a form of manipulation with the 3 that would create the struggle or conflict, until resolved.

In life, the 4's mere presence is healing; part of the reason why they are only one out of every twenty-five people. In a relationship, the 4 tends to be the emotional anchor, not just for a partnership but for the whole family or group. The 4 tends to hold the emotional energy, so the 3 can be as powerful as they wish, but the 4 is reflecting back to the 3 the emotional component of their life and the emotional contents of the decisions the 3 came to make.

Most 3's are very good at procrastinating the right use of their power to make emotional decisions. The reason is that emotional decisions compel them to face their greatest fear - that they really are uniquely *that* powerful. If a 3, on some higher level of their being, elects to be with a 4 either in a karmic family or intimate relationship, what do you suppose will happen along the way? The 4 will represent to the 3 that qualitative aspect of the higher Self of the 3 that is rooted in the lesson of learning how to make emotional decisions, and will in some manner cause those lessons to externalize in the life-path of the 3.

Can you see how inevitable it is that we create our own lessons in the personage of the people we encounter in life? Can you see the intricate tapestry of the universe at work?

Some 3's give away their power in order to avoid conflict (conflict does not always mean violence, it means the pairs of opposites: yes/no, up/down, black/white, etc.). The conflict is what helps the 3 define their emotional decisions.

The 4 reflects to the 3 that there are many forms of power; that not all power is visible and massive. First, 4's can help 3's to accept themselves as powerful and to externalize that power in gentle ways. The king is king. No one ever argues whether the king is king. The question for the 3 is "What kind of king are you?"

It is not whether you have power, it is "How will you use it?" Are there kind and gentle ways to display power? Of course. Paramhansa Yogananda was a consummate third chakra personality. How do you suppose he put forth the right use of his power?

But second and more importantly, is the Feminine Principle, which the 4 is meant to live as a quality of being. In essence, the Feminine Principle is using the power of the will to allow, instead of to push. It is yielding with the heart (feelings) to what the mind cannot yet know. It is a ferocity of trust to allow your Self to be the essence of your God-Self, without having to push on a door that is meant to open inwards. In other words, you do not ascend to God, you bring God to you by realizing you are that.

You do not evolve into higher levels of consciousness as much as you allow your Self to be all consciousness, because in reality there are no levels, only the mind's desire to construct a meaningful universe where levels of attainment signify personal growth. "Be still, and know that I am God," it says in the Bible. "The kingdom of heaven is within you" is also from the Bible. If you truly live in a Oneness, how can you be separate from what you seek?

In the case of the 3, the 4 is showing the Feminine Principle as a matter of their being in this lifetime. In all cases, the better each individual does in life, the more effective they can be in helping others, simply because they exist.

Remember again, please, we exist in *all* our chakras. They are qualitative emanations, localized space-time continuum events that are higher expressions (still us) flowing consciousness into this dimension. We may just tend to favor one expression over the others to learn those particular lessons.

EVEN/EVEN AND ODD/ODD-NUMBERED DOMINANT CHAKRAS:
WHAT HAPPENS WHEN THEY GET TOGETHER

Head swimming yet? Well, it's important to cover all the major conventional bases when discussing relationship pairs. In this case, you have two yin-type or two yang-type chakra dominant persons, just not the same chakra. As you'll see, same-chakra relationships can be either really good or really challenging.

Such pairings can be:

2-4 yin/yin

2-6 yin/yin

4-6 yin/yin

3-5 yang/yang

I've picked a few of the more common examples to demonstrate the energetics that happen in consciousness in these relationships.

The level and intensity changes with the level of intimacy. That means that a 2-4 relationship would be quite different in a workplace setting compared to an intimate setting.

2-4 RELATIONSHIP

Here we begin to get into the same type of feminine energy principle among two chakras. Since we've discussed much of the qualities of the 2 and 4 earlier, we can concentrate more on the interactions. Keep in mind that "feminine" as well as "masculine" refers to the way a consciousness externalizes their soul quality through their waking personality, *not the sex of the person.*

You may imagine how similar energy components of chakras are no longer complementary as in classic 5-2 or 3-4 combinations of yin and yang chakras. Instead we have two yin or feminine quality chakras.

Chakras 2 and 4 are very emotionally based. Chakra 6 is also emotionally based, but much less connected to physical reality of the quality of what love is. That is, the creativity, passion, viscerality, love, lust, empathy, sexuality and sensuality flow as a quality of consciousness more through chakras 2 and 4 than through chakras 3, 5, or 6.

When there is a relationship between a 2 and a 4, there is much possibility that the emotional component is both a blessing and a challenge.

The 2 reflects back to the 4 creativity, infinite alternatives, and passion. Where the 4 is rooted in love, the 2 is rooted in passion. The 2 is the way-shower, the pioneer of new vistas and the explorer where no path before existed. The 2 reflects to the 4 new ways of doing things, of how to express love and desire, of an inner knowingness that there really are choices and opportunities.

The 2 reflects to the 4 the passion of life, the desire for sensual and emotional depth and connection, both for the big picture and the extreme details. The second chakra person sometimes likes it all! The 2 shows the 4 the vibrant colors and weave of the many threads in the tapestry of life; what there is that's worth living for, what there is when desire and passion for life burst forth like a field of wildflowers.

As the 4 must learn to be the emotional communicator and to accept as much love as they give, so also can the 2 help the 4 to find the passion to do so, to love themselves as fiercely as they love others.

Just as a 5 needs to be *physically* grounded to the earth plane, the 4 person needs to be *emotionally* grounded. A passionate and alive 2 can help with this, especially if they are in the higher aspect of their chakra, by showing the 4 what is worth living for. Remember, some 2's experience great pain so they can know great joy, then they teach that experience as a quality (consciousness) of their being to the world.

The 2 reflects back to the 4 the bigger expression, the higher vision, as so many 4's don't have a good idea of their own personal identity. This is because the 4 can be so very empathic to others' feelings that they assume the feelings are their own. Some 4's spend a lifetime separating their own feelings from those of others, and have only slowly learned healthy emotional boundaries over much time.

A person can lament, "How come it has taken so much time for me to learn this lesson?" Because you keep the lesson with you as long as the illusion is with you. Remember the catch-22 is that the only way to overcome an illusion is to first recognize that there is one. In other words, as you become more evolved, you automatically become aware of those patterns of behavior that no longer serve you. Your perception/will/reaction changes.

The 4 reflects back to the 2 the quality of what love is, without condition. Many 2's succumb to doubt, guilt, regret, remorse and more, because their fundamental fear is that they cannot create anything greater than that which came before. This is an illusion, as are those that the mind lives from all the chakras, but a very good illusion. Those same 2's work themselves half to death to validate their existence as "good enough." But what if a 2 is with a 4 who is emanating love and purity? Could a 2 accept it? Sometimes, yes. Sometimes, no.

Some people have difficulty living with a good person, as hard as that is to grasp. Perhaps you are a person, reading this book, who has had a relationship that had mistrust and doubt. When you ended that relationship, was it easy for you to go on to another relationship where your partner was trustworthy and honest, and was it easy for you to accept? Once our trust is abused, it is difficult to trust again. Some people do not.

The 4 can bring a peacefulness to the 2 that accepts whatever the 2 creates as good enough, and helps them validate themselves as whole and complete, not needing the 4 for completion, but desiring a wholesome companionship based on trust and fidelity.

Sometimes the 2 can get caught up in the hysteria of the uncertainty of their own future. Remember, the 2 can predict how others can be as whole and complete, just not for themselves because they must learn trust and faith in the Self. 2's can become addictive, can access the passive-aggressive, codependent, enabling, and even vindictive parts of themselves to establish some form of security, some form of predictability, because they have fallen into the pit of chaos that is in the lower aspect of the second chakra.

The 4 can reflect back the unending quality that love represents to the 2. Many 4's underestimate their purity, just as many 2's underestimate their preciousness. So the pairing of 2's and 4's can help establish more emotional grounding for the 4 in the purity they represent and more accepting of the sacredness and faith in Self that the 2 seeks.

5-3 RELATIONSHIP

The 5-3 relationship is to the masculine principle, as the 4-2 is to the feminine. Sometimes powerful chakras pair for their mutual growth. It would be a mistake to think that chakras 2 and 4 are not powerful. They are, just in a different expression of consciousness along the lines of the Feminine Principle.

The outgoing nature of the masculine energy of the 5 and 3 also means demonstrative power, rather more of an externalization to know the explanation or flow of consciousness and the truth of it, respectively.

So, perhaps in the manner in which a 2-4 challenge each other emotionally, the 5-3 will challenge each other to act towards acceptance of their mental and will-based gifts, in a feeling sense that can then be externalized as emotions.

As we have detailed much of what the 5 and 3 represent earlier, we can concentrate on their reflections here.

A 3 reflects back to the 5 the value in being grounded. A 5 can "choose" a 3 to bring some power struggles into their life or to challenge each other as to who can "best work and agree." That is, they can spiritually challenge each other to greater understandings of life and its workings, as the fifth chakra person has been called the "step-down transformer for God" and the third chakra person the hierophant (spiritual seeker).

The 3 reflects back to the 5 the essence of personal power, but sometimes lacks the emotional component of trust that the 5 is seeking. If the 5 is evolved and balanced, the reflection becomes an enhancement to induce the 5 to individualize their explanations for how the universe works and how to transmit their knowledge to humanity in a manner that is understandable.

The 5 needs to understand how to speak and teach on different levels. Buddha was very fifth chakra dominant. In his teachings, he would have a higher, more esoteric level that he taught his inner circle of students. To the rest of humanity, he taught a simplified version. Was Buddha holding back on society? Was he holding something over their heads? In true metaphysics, no one can hold anything over your head. Since you live in a Oneness, you are a part of all Will, Love and Wisdom.

The 3 awakens that it is OK for the 5 to be powerful, that teachings can have many levels and complexities, and that it may be necessary to have one level of teaching for one group, and another level for another group. One of the telepathic strengths of 5's is the ability to "match frequencies" with the person to whom they are communicating. It is essential, since part of their soul's purpose is to increase comprehension and understanding in the world: hence the name "step-down transformer for God." Fifth chakra people must remember that true teachers will always desire that their students exceed all their teachings.

The 3 reflects back to the 5 what personal power is, to take responsibility for the fact that it is not only OK to be powerful, it is a part of who we are. By representing the power to articulate what humanity cannot yet understand, 5's are in even more service to the very people they seek to help.

The 3 also reflects back to the 5 the value of articulating the truth. What if you are attempting to explain a great truth to someone who is not yet ready to understand it? Would you still have communicated it, nonetheless? Would the other person get it? The point is that 5's must learn to articulate their teachings as well as they can, and know when to let go when no understanding is possible.

The 3's can sometimes appear arrogant in their higher aspect, because they are willing to live a level of truth and have the veracity to be genuine in its exposition to the world. They're not really arrogant, but it can seem so in the same manner that very evolved people can seem detached from the people they are teaching. It is a choice of attachment, not an arrogance or distancing.

But there are times when the 5 really will be the only person in the room who knows what's going on. Since we all have fifth chakras, perhaps you've felt this way at times? The 3 helps the 5 to hold the value of their teachings in all the higher aspects of what the fifth chakra represents.

The 5 reflects back to the 3 how to measure the quality of their truth through careful articulation of its power to others. That is, the 3 learns from the 5 to understand their power, not just that they are in fact powerful.

As the 3 represents truth, power, and uniqueness, the 3 helps the 5 to take the understanding that they've learned and then how to be authentic and genuine (unique) with the knowledge. As one of the lower aspects of the third chakra is to compare themselves to others, the 3 learns how to individuate their power and stay away from comparisons, and also they emanate that quality to the fifth chakra person. Teachings from an authentic teacher. Unique teachings. Imagine that. What could make a 5 more effective? *Grounding.*

The rational and practical nature that often accompanies the 3's personality helps to ground the 5. Most 5's do not like being grounded onto the earth plane, because if they are grounded they can feel, and if they can feel they can feel pain. That same power of the 3 to get to the point or bottom line can help the 5 to see the value in a grounded approach and leave the daydreaming "head in the clouds" lack of grounding they so often suffer from. As before, these are life issues. Being grounded is something the 5 will work on for life. But being grounded helps make the life of a 5 more productive, efficacious, and meaningful.

Many 3's have issues with anger because they are sensitive to the iniquities and injustices that exist in the world. Those same 3's often do not know they have anger, misplace its true meaning, or hold onto it for such a long time that it externalizes as a medical condition, usually related to digestion, solid or hollow organs in the mid-body, or hormonal system/biochemistry of the body. (For more on physical manifestations of illnesses related to the chakras, see <u>Eye of the Lotus: *Psychology of the Chakras*</u>.)

The 3 is often the skeptic, though in a good way. That means a 3 is willing to ask the tough questions that no one else is willing to, not out of fear but out of a desire to know the truth. Third chakra skeptics are my favorite people.

These are powerful associations that we choose on higher levels of our being. The general examples are a fraction of the infinite combinations and complexities with which we interact in our reflections and reciprocities with others.

SAME-CHAKRA DOMINANT RELATIONSHIPS:
WHAT HAPPENS WHEN THEY GET TOGETHER

What happens when two of the same chakra types, say a 5 and a 5, get together? It is often like the analogy of two magnets. Hold their north and south ends close, and they click together. Hold both north ends close to each other, and they repel. In other words, it can be really, really good, or really, really bad. But there are many exceptions and permutations that come about in the relationship.

It depends on the evolution of the individuals, but the pendulum of possibilities can swing from extreme to extreme through the higher and lower aspects of the chakras of same-chakra relationships.

The good thing is that all pendulums swing through the center on the way to the extremes, so there is the possibility of each person "coming to center" in the relationship.

The real question is: "Why would two of the same-chakra types come together?" For the same reason as any other relationship: Life is about the development of character, not about goals or the accumulation of material things.

If you attract a same-chakra person to you, there is a pertinent karmic or life lesson to be met and learned.

Such pairings can be:

2-2 yin/yin

3-3 yang/yang

4-4 yin/yin

5-5 yang/yang

6-6 yin/yin

I've seen all pairings, except the 6-6. It's rare enough to find even one person who is dominant in their sixth chakra, let alone a person who would pair with a similar dominant chakra. Rare, but possible.

2-2 RELATIONSHIP

When a couple of 2's get together, it can be the passionate romance of the century, the most vindictive, knock-down, drag-out "I'm gonna get mine no matter what" scenario, or most often, a watered-down version somewhere in between. The reason is in the chakra itself. Everyone has second chakra issues, whether they are dominant in that chakra or not.

Why? Because it is more connected to the five senses than any other chakra. I call it the visceral chakra. So, 2's are rooted in a deep desire for feeling the meaning of life, the passion of living, the externalization of the sensory input that fuels their visionary apparatus to psychically "see over the horizon" what the rest of us are only dimly aware of.

One of the examples I've observed involves a 2-2 relationship where the married couple are both psychologists. As you'll see from the case history, pairing same chakra types can be very challenging, and hopefully it can answer some questions you may have about the chakra-dominant types of people you have in your life in their various roles.

Since two of the same chakra come to do the same things and to learn the same things, what is the benefit of meeting?

The first and most obvious answer is that *one of them may be very much more evolved than the other.* There may be a parental, familial or intimate karmic connection. There also may be the desire to fan the flames of the passion for living that, in this case, two 2's can accomplish by being in each other's lives.

The 2's come to learn faith in their own vision, to not spread themselves too thin, and to fully accept themselves by, in part, receiving the love and goodness that they offer to the world. If 2's pair, they have the potential for intimate knowledge of their strengths and weaknesses if they are willing to do the inspirational inner work necessary to overcome the guilt and chaos.

If they are not willing to work at it, both can be quite unaware of the dynamics that prolong the feelings of emotional overwhelm, hostage to one's emotions of guilt, hurtful exchanges when none is necessary.

This dance of consciousness is sometimes like a ride at Disneyland. You go through the dark tunnel together, not always knowing what doors will open or which way you'll turn, but you're doing it together. A mutual dance of faith; a ferocity of trust in your Self where you would never underestimate who you truly are, yet always desire what is beyond the next door. If both of you are mature emotionally, you can weather the changes. If not, you'll both bob like corks on the seas of emotion, tossed about by every wave from every direction.

Equanimity means to choose to be calm, even when things and/or people around you are not calm. Sogyal Rinpoche in The Tibetan Book of Living and Dying speaks of meditation in terms of sinking down below the ocean of waves, deeper in the ocean of your mind. You can be aware of the waves, but not affected by them because you are in a deeper place.

When the 2's reach emotional equanimity, they are in a place of inner calm. Sogyal explains that in meditation, the sun has rays and the ocean has waves. It is very much like the mind to think anyway, but you can choose not to be affected by its "waves." So it is with the second chakras emotional passion. It is like the 2 to have waves of passion for life, but you can go to a deeper place and not be so affected by the tossing waves of emotions, a place of calm, a place of equanimity. A pair of 2's can achieve this if they are willing to work on emotional maturity.

When the 2's are in a place of pedantic attitudes, reverse chaotic manipulation, vindictiveness, or passive-aggressive behavior, watch out. The second chakra, more than the others, can be the root cause of tremendous self-destruction, and a second chakra person can pull you down with them into an endless pit of neediness based on their fundamental fear (that they cannot create anything greater than that which came before) that gives rise to all the abandonment, abuse, and abundance issues. The desire for approval and the fear of rejection are based on abandonment issues that come forth through the second chakra.

The seeds of all these problems exist in all of us, though they may never surface, according to our life paths.

Sometimes thought to be born ahead of their time, 2's can build tremendous visions of the future. They are the bringers of the dawn of tomorrow, and are sometimes rejected by the very people they wish to serve because the vision is too grand to comprehend. Ironically, sometimes it is easer to shoot the messenger than it is to read the message and understand it. Our history is full of luminaries who have sought to bring us great visions, and some of them have suffered terribly for it. Part of the message is to hang onto your vision, no matter how well it is received or how much it is rejected.

The 2's can build upon each other's ability to see over the horizon by reflecting back to each other ever-higher visions of what could be. Remember the second chakra also represents infinite creativity and alternatives. The reverse of that is faithlessness or hopelessness; no choice, no alternatives. 2's can reject the illusion and offer gifts to the world of the "new tomorrow" that is, in fact, an accurate possibility if others are willing to take the leap of faith as well, as much as the 2's already have.

Living within the ocean of possibilities also presents the problem of great overwhelm: knowing which possibility to choose and knowing it is the right one. A pair of 2's can, through mutual and regular inspiration and spiritual practices, build a strong foundation of the visionary, the new direction where there was no path before, only a feeling that was trusted through inner faith in the vision.

The true vision? The one shown you in your inspirations. And they both will represent that to the world through the 95% of communication that is the energy of consciousness.

5-5 RELATIONSHIP

When two 5's get together, the basic dynamics of same-chakra interaction you saw above apply: both dominant chakra persons are here to do and to learn similar experiences that will help define the nature of their character in this lifetime.

But how would it be of help to pair with another 5, when a fifth chakra person must, for life, always work on being grounded (reminding their metaphysical nature that they have a corporeal presence, one of the Hermetic principles, As Above – So Below)? Since all the chakras are always working, no one is in just one chakra all the time, and fifth chakra people in general will always encounter some lessons that stimulate their second chakra's visceral nature to help them ground in this dimension.

A 5 can reflect back to a 5 what happens when one is not grounded. That is, think of your Self as a person who has a "piling system" instead of a neat filing system at home. You have lots of things to do, but your piles of papers and stuff keep stacking up. Say you meet another person whose piling system makes yours look like nothing. The first and natural reaction would be that you're really not so bad off, that your situation, by comparison, is nothing compared to the other person. But what it does is draw attention to your condition of why the piling system exists in the first place.

If a contemplative person contemplates, what would tend to be the outcome? More contemplation, to be sure, but solely within that person. If two contemplative people meet and work together, even a slight difference of thought can be the key to significant change. In this universe, sometimes the smallest turn of our cheeks toward a change in our perceptions can make the biggest changes in our lives.

It could be that a certain 5 may respond only to nuances and not to the grossness (rough and uneven energy) that can sometimes be experienced by the fifth chakra person. By having another fifth chakra person reflect those same nuances back perhaps it is the key manner in which they may perceive the possibility of a change or a new way of looking at things.

Perhaps sometimes the teacher is the hardest person to teach, unless it is by another teacher. Perhaps another 5, through nuance, can instill the desire to be grounded in a fifth chakra person. Perhaps the lesson is a momentary pairing of the two 5's for mutual grounding.

In the past two centuries, Western philosophers wrestled with the problem of language. They argued that language, like the English you are reading, is based on symbols and as such is a highly ineffective form of communication. The fifth chakra person comes to the earth plane to give meaning and comprehension, to burst past the limitations of symbology. Imagine the difficulty of breaking those illusions with a population of people inured in that same symbology. Imagine knowing, within your heart, that you have the skills to help people understand what they yet cannot, to help articulate to humanity what it cannot yet comprehend. That is a fifth chakra person.

By pairing with another 5, they can reinforce in each other the desire, capability, and psychic acuity (remember they are both telepathic, by definition) to reaffirm their soul's purpose as teacher/communicators. If 5's were called healers, then they would be healing comprehension and understanding in people, though it is wise to remember that not all people are ready, willing, or able to understand. As mentioned, even Buddha had two levels of teachings.

The 5's as a pair can reinforce their ability to step down the teachings into a palatable form for the particular soul-group to which they are led. "When the students are ready, the teacher appears." But also, "When the teacher is ready, the students appear." Part of the journey of the 5 personality is being led to various, diverse groups of people to help overcome their limited ideas of reality; to help overcome the illusion of separation as to why those groups of people should be separate from any other group.

The like-minded 5's can find solace and support in each other, but inevitably they must both work diligently on being grounded constantly, and guarding with great awareness against the mentalisms that plague the fifth chakra personality, and thus result in the emotional unavailability that so many 5's suffer from.

If they engage in spiritual practices, such as prayer and meditation, it will give them a firm base from which to live (as it would any chakra dominance). Particularly, yoga practices (there are many forms, but any form that has a true yogi-breathing technique) are most helpful because the breathing practice, along with the forms, provides a steady, grounded base for the fifth chakra person to feel productive and efficacious in this lifetime. Doing so will also render them most emotionally available to others with whom they associate.

How would a pair of 5's help each other to learn the life's lesson of trusting their feelings? If you recall, a 5, like any other person, has feelings already but the 5 tends to stay in the mind because of the strength of the fifth chakra, as dominant. How would such a pair engender trust in feelings; to trust with their heart what their mind cannot yet know?

Inherent in each of us, regardless of chakra dominance, is an infallible mechanism that seeks balance, and this is how we draw others to us who represent the externalization of the balance we seek. If you think about it, within you is perfection, Oneness. Therefore, anything that is imperfect is instantly noticeable.

If you have the illusion of needing to be in your mind to cope with the exigencies of the third dimension, it is natural that you would seek comfort there. But, since it is already an illusion, that within you would seek balance, and can find it in interactions (reflections) with another person, even another 5.

Remember, the greatest fear for fifth chakra people is that no one will ever know them for who they really are. Partly it is because the vibration of the fifth chakra is very fine and very high. But it is also because the fifth chakra stimulates the physical mind with the criteria "to know." Who would know a 5 better than another fifth chakra person?

SUMMARY OF TYPICAL CHAKRA-TYPE RELATIONSHIPS

What we see is a lifetime of challenges based on our chakra dominance. The people who come into our lives who represent the reciprocity or reflection of our soul's desire, are necessary elements of our growth. We were meant to work together.

What I have written is a mere drop in the possible universe of combinations of different chakra types interacting and reflecting back the wholeness that they already represent as individuated aspects of the creative mind of God.

Hopefully I've whet your appetite to learn more about your Self, your reflections and reciprocities, the people in your life, all pointing the way "home."

Don't look immediately to place your Self in just one chakra: you may find that by seeing a little of your Self in them that you really are composed of all chakras, all consciousness.

But perhaps in this lifetime, you are focused in certain areas. That is your karma and your dharma.

You are in the chakra gym. Nothing will change unless you work out in the gym and overcome your illusions, learn what you came to learn, and do what you came to do. It is the effort, not the goal, which defines your character in a given lifetime. Just make the effort.

CHAPTER 8

THE KEYS TO A GREAT RELATIONSHIP

Following are a simple set of keys for creating and maintaining great relationships, whether they are social, work-related, family, or intimate. If you use these techniques, you will see definite results. No relationship is perfect. It does take work, but it can be a great work of art.

REFLECTIONS OF GOD

Everyone you meet is in some way a reflection of you. *Every one.* As a dear friend of mine would say: "We are all spectral reflections of our Selves." How you react to your reflections (even not reacting is a reaction) is a definition of your character.

Through your free will, you make the choices that define your life, and the ones to follow this one, in an unfolding sequence to bring you back into the heart and mind of the Creator, whole and complete.

Knowing that everyone around you is in some way pointing a finger towards God gives you the opportunity to see how
that may be. It does not mean you analyze every relationship.
Rather, behold the beauty of this universe to bring you every
opportunity, through your relationships, to "look for the open
energy"; a second chakra phrase that offers you an ever-
renewing way to seek the light in every situation, and by
so doing overcome the illusion that causes suffering.

It has been said that those who are conscious are alert to
the opportunities the universe represents. Look for how best
to develop these opportunities in your relationships. Look for
the open energy in your reflections. Understand that your
part in it is part of the elegance of life to unfold as the flower
does, to its fullest and most beautiful potential: The expression of God you were meant to be.

EMOTIONAL COMMUNICATION

Any true relationship is built on communication, but
emotional communication is different than just conveying
information to each other. It's difficult to communicate accurately your intent emotionally. Did you ever watch a soap
opera and hear when the woman says to her boyfriend, "You
know I love you, but I'm not *in* love with you"? What does *that*
mean? How can you quantify love?

But we do it all the time. We try to convey the meaning of
our emotions, at times, as if they were as quantifiable as a
pound of apples. It is because the essence of love is a quality
that it cannot be quantified. It is a state of being that we
experience.

Have you ever fallen in love, and do you remember that
feeling? Did you ever hold a baby and have a feeling of deep

love and protection for that baby? How did you *know* what you felt? And yet, you know what you're feeling. It is absolutely *not* the same thing as thinking. Thinking is linear; feeling is not.

When communicating your emotions, be as clear as you can be. Don't tell the other person what to do, tell them what you are *feeling*. Do it as fully and completely as you can. Remember that our language represents a problem in that it is based on symbols. It's hard enough just to convey information, let alone emotions!

Use phrases such as "I feel," or "My feeling is," or "I sense," or "My sense is," or "My desires are," when communicating your feelings. This is important for two reasons: You're not telling the person what you think, but what you *feel*, and you are only offering information – you are not telling them what to do or what to think. So often in emotional communication a person can feel like they are being given an ultimatum or being told what to do. The person can overreact in emotional overwhelm, shutting down any real possible communication between you.

Using these phrases shows great respect for the other person on your part, and it also shows the depth of your own commitment to *your* feelings. You cannot always know what the other person is feeling. You cannot always know exactly what you are feeling, but you can start from what you are sensing. Saying nothing will leave the other person guessing.

Ask someone who has been dating or who has had one or more divorces what is the greatest lesson they've learned, and invariably it will be "To be a better emotional communicator."

Remember that you do have higher sense perceptions. Everyone does, but not everyone is aware that they exist or how to use them. It all begins with trust, a fierce inner trust in your ability to know the truth of your being. The more you are willing to be vulnerable to your own growth, to your heart's (soul's) desires, the more you will awaken those higher senses. At first it may be a little confusing, as the higher senses do not work in the same way as your five physical senses do.

Imagine if you are clear in your heart and tuned into your higher sense perceptions how much better your emotional communication will be.

With practice, trust, and more trust, you will see the higher expression of your Self proceed forth in a graceful manner of true spiritual growth. This will definitely have an effect on all your relationships, be they work, social, or intimate. Be willing to trust with your heart and you can form great relationships.

Bear in mind that you can do everything "right" and still not have a particular relationship work, because it takes both wills to be in alignment, and you only have power over yours. Do the best you can. That is all anyone could ask.

As you awaken your higher sense perceptions, you'll see people as they really are, not what they project to you. Be compassionate in the way that they choose to be, but also have healthy emotional boundaries and do not be afraid to communicate those boundaries. How could you hope to have a great relationship if your partner does not know what your boundaries are? Again, don't make them guess. Be direct, yet gentle, if you have to.

One last word. If you *really desire* to get your point across, *touch* people and look them in the eyes. Don't stare them down; just let them see the sincerity in your heart through your eyes. Touching and eye contact together really get another person's attention. Be very gentle and respectful of this technique. It is very powerful.

HEALTHY EMOTIONAL BOUNDARIES

If you're already good at emotional communication, continue and let your partner, sibling, boss, etc., know your healthy emotional boundaries. It is essential that you communicate them, but the level of communication changes with the venue. You would not communicate the same intimacy in a work environment that you would with your spouse or partner. Appropriate communication is important; knowing what your boundaries are is just as important.

What if you are slightly confused and aren't quite sure what your boundaries are? How would you know? One way is to practice moments of inspiration (see Spiritual Practices later in this chapter). Regular inspiration awakens your higher sense perceptions, using one or more of your five senses to stimulate your feelings to your soul's desires. Doing so gives you personal clarity, increases your sense of your own sacredness and things that are private and holy to you, and helps you to form them into a boundary of what you will and will not accept.

If you are a woman, my experience in counseling is that men do not take hints. Be very clear in your communication of your boundaries. Even ask: "Repeat back to me what you think I just said" if you need to. Better for you to be clear than to make assumptions.

If you are a man, don't be fearful to approach a woman and express your feelings. Do you know how many women would love to hear how their man feels; the real feelings of his heart?

And, there are infinite numbers of variations and approaches in relationships. My advice is to trust your *feelings* and use your best judgment.

Of course, the feeling of the moment will help you to best convey what your boundaries are. But also, a boundary is not only a type of fence you put up that says what you will and won't accept. A boundary also gives you a *yard* in which to be your Self. A safe place of repose in your integrity. A knowingness that you are in fidelity to that which is sacred and holy within you.

Remember to use the "My feeling is" statements when you are expressing your boundaries.

AUTHENTICITY

Using the eye contact and touching communication technique above, what do you think the result would be if you were not authentic? Genuineness comes from fidelity to your inner truth; getting real with your Self and your expectations in a relationship.

Let's take a step back, for a moment. Remember that in all communication, 95% is energy? Remember that the people you draw to you, by the Law of Reciprocity, are the reflections of God in your life? They are the reflections of the balance you seek that was incepted by the flawless inner-knowing, the God-Self of "perfected-ness" that you already possess.

That being true, can you see how important it is to be totally authentic with your Self first, before you contact or commit with someone else? If a little voice within you is saying "something is wrong," then something is probably wrong.

Authenticity means being, saying, and acting in accordance with your inner truth. If truth is truth, how come we're not all the same? Because we individuate the truth *uniquely*, relative to our current capability and capacity to hold and understand it.

None of us acts in absolute truth, though we hold it within us. We all operate in relative, subjective truth. That is, we hold the truth we do, until we obtain a higher awareness of a greater truth. What we hold as true today may shift in the light of higher awareness tomorrow.

Therefore, to be authentic means to hold in fidelity the inner truth we do have, to the best of our ability. We all externalize the truth of our nature differently; that does not make it wrong or right. We all hold a little piece of the mirror of truth, and we hold up that mirror for everyone we meet. Better for us if our own mirror is clean and highly polished!

We all have different ways of externalizing our truth. In Autobiography of a Yogi, Paramhansa Yogananda speaks of a guru in India whose meditative practice was to go into the jungle, find a tiger, and wrestle it! Imagine, that was his meditation. I don't suppose we all need to wrestle tigers today as our meditation, but we all do have ways of addressing the truth that emanates from our center.

Let it be unique to you - that's OK. Just let it be the honest you. One of the worst things you could do in a relationship is surrender that authenticity in order to preserve or harmonize the relationship. How would it serve your partner to surrender your own truth? What, then, would you be reflecting back to them? A lower level of truth? You cannot help anyone from a position of weakness. Ghandi said: "We must be the change we seek in the world." He did not say *become* or *almost be*. Think about it.

Be authentic with others. They will benefit more from your veracity and genuineness. Don't be the idea of the other person's perfection. Be what you are. If you love to wrestle tigers for your meditation, so be it. If you're a biker who is also a holistic energy practitioner, so be it. If you're a beautiful model who knows Kung Fu, so be it. Just be genuine.

So many people fall into the trap of trying to be what the other person wants. In the U.S. there is tremendous pressure in pop culture to look and act a certain way, to have certain things, and so on. For years women and girls have suffered from eating disorders because they are trying to be the image of what they think will make them attractive and accepted.

Today, many young men are also suffering from anorexia, or weight lift to extremes to become the idea of what they believe is attractive. If you like being a certain body type, do it because it comes from your authentic core and for no outside reason.

The fact that marketers and advertisers play to that energy constantly through print and electronic media only fuels the flames of illusion. And we are victims of the illusion, as long as we allow it to be so.

AVAILABILITY

You must be open to the possibility of great relationships; *you must be emotionally available to receive great love.* Remember that you can do everything right and still it might not work out, due to the free will of the other person.

To be open in your heart and to allow is to be emotionally available. Allow does not mean "allow anything" or not to have healthy emotional boundaries. It means to kindle the flames that illuminate the temple of your own sacredness, your own holiness, that you could know great love that *already* exists within you. That means, as the Feminine Principle states, to use the power of your will to allow your Self to *receive* as much love as that which you *give*.

So many of us are capable and do give such great love to others, but we sometimes are emotionally starved ourselves. Why? Because, partly, it is easier to give than to receive. To give requires no vulnerability. To receive does, because we cannot always control the content or the outcome. The terrible "T" word *trust* enters here as a necessary part of your evolution by the manner in which you trust so completely in your inner perfection, that by opening to the possibility to receive great love, you can.

Without the fierce love of your Self, you cannot awaken the awareness of your inner perfection to your conscious mind. It is not Self love like secular humanism, but the love of the Divine Spark that glows within you, that you are made in the image of the Creator, including all love, already existing within you.

There is nothing to create; only to allow to come forth that which already exists within you. Trust that it is there, with all your being. The more you recognize your true spiritual nature, the more you overcome the illusion of separation.

When in an intimate relationship, here are three simple questions you can ask your Self to see if you really are emotionally available:

1. Is my partner sending me as much love as I am giving him or her? (This is not a contest, just a question to get you to be honest about whether your partner really is offering and giving you love.)

2. If my partner is sending me love, am I open and

available to receive it? (Be honest. Are you sitting still long enough to let your partner love you? Are you quieting your mind when together to allow your Self to receive love?)

3. If I am open and available to receive love, am I actually receiving it? (Are you allowing it to happen, to let the moment be a drop of total consciousness; a universe in itself, composed entirely of love? Have you surrendered to your Self, your inner trust, that you could be loved that deeply?)

You cannot make someone love you. If you feel great love from another, it is partly because you have allowed your Self to *feel* it, and partly because the profundity of such great love already exists within you perfectly, whole and complete, and partly because you *are* that love, incarnate.

SPIRITUAL PRACTICES

Spiritual practices are an elementary and necessary part of a healthy existence that help our lives become meaningful and productive. They are a respect and recognition for those beneficial forces in the universe that are beyond our mind's comprehension, but within the grasp of our hearts.

These practices help focus an individual on the central and important themes of life: compassion, harmlessness, meaningfulness, productivity. Such practices benefit all forms of relationships greatly for obvious reasons.

Spiritual practices include, but are not limited to:

*   *Mindfulness* – Fully being present in every moment. Considering that every moment of time contains a drop of total consciousness. God provides – man decides.

- *Prayer* - Prayer is like talking to God, asking for dispensations, relief of karma, illusion, and suffering. Paramhansa Yogananda said: "God loves to have His skirt tugged on by us." That means there's nothing wrong with being eager and enthusiastic about spiritual growth and understanding of our true nature.

- *Meditation* - Sogyal Rinpoche said: "In the clear sky, there are no clouds." The clear sky is our true nature. The clouds, while puffy and beautiful, are like our thoughts. They can obscure our vision from the clear sky of our true being. Meditation is like listening to God. Sometimes, God speaks in the softest whisper of an angel's breath upon our cheeks. If we are not quiet and still, we miss the subtle cues that God is sending us.

- *Yoga Practices* - Yoga, in its many forms, "tonifies" the body, balances the chakras, calms the breathing and the mind, and sets a powerful stage for true spiritual growth. In my book Eye of the Lotus: *Psychology of the Chakras*, there are wonderful Hatha (gentle, traditional) yoga exercises by powerful yoga school director Madhu Honeymann.

- *Inspiration* - Watching a sunset, beholding the mountain meadow, sitting in the audience of a symphony orchestra: we all have something that inspires us. Inspiration is similar to listening to music. Music requires no thought to know if we like it because the music goes straight to the emotions. Inspiration uses one or more of the five senses to kindle the desires of the soul brightly enough that we can perceive them and feel their intensity. Inspiration requires no thought, only your vulnerability to feel through your senses. Regular inspiration, even if only for minutes, has two hidden benefits: you get your *identity* back (a sense of life's direction); and you get your *integrity* back (healthy emotional boundaries).

HOW TO EVOLVE YOURSELF SPIRITUALLY

Any real attempt to evolve yourself to a greater level of spiritual awareness must include two things:

1. Awaken the chakras
2. Live in faith

With any spiritual practice there must be some rigor, some dedication to the principles of higher awareness based on love, compassion, and harmlessness. When I am training healers, we always start with a guided meditation in which I say "May the principles of harmlessness and compassion be the guide of your every thought and action."

Awakening the chakras includes purification of each one. This can be done with yoga philosophy and yoga practices, prayer, and dharma (right living, right action, right relationship).

There are teachings you can study where you can understand that your chakras exist in the higher dimensions as well as this one, and that they can be awakened in the physical, astral, and causal dimensions.

Each level of awakening represents a higher level of awareness and the overcoming of illusion. Can you imagine seeing someone as they are and not as they appear to be?

The awakening process throughout life is very similar to the Japanese concept of "Budo" as applied to martial arts: training that is relentless and unending. There is no goal as important as the effort made to get there.

Secondly, faith must always be in place. *Faith means trusting with your heart what your mind cannot yet know.* Faith is your reach extending beyond your grasp, for you must reach beyond your understanding, beyond what you can conceive and imagine. Faith evokes the humorous anecdote: "If you knew what an epiphany was, it wouldn't be one."

Faith is an essential part of one's character. Living a life of faith is difficult, personal, and intimate. No one can do it for you. It is so essential to never assume that you know everything, for the material mind cannot.

Information is not knowledge, knowledge is not wisdom, and wisdom is not awareness. As you aspire to higher levels of awareness, be content that in the moment you know enough. It is in the moment that faith dwells, not in the future.

As you live in faith, you awaken your higher sense perceptions. The higher sense perceptions do not work in the same way as the five senses, and therefore it can feel a little awkward or confusing when trusting them.

But as you awaken your higher sense perceptions, you start to see things as they are, not as they appear to be. *And the only way you can truly help others is to evolve yourself.*

Awakening the chakras, and a life of faith, are both essential for true spiritual growth beyond a belief.

Prayer and meditation without faith is just thinking.

Yoga without faith is just stretching.

CHAPTER 9

GET OUT OF THE POOL:
HOW TO PREVENT EMOTIONAL OVERWHELM

It's funny how when we're presented with problems in the everyday world, they are mostly easy to solve... unless they involve the emotions. Emotional problems bring in words like values, morals, boundaries, ethics, and desires – all qualities that are difficult to quantify and reduce to practical measures.

Emotional overwhelm. I'm sure you have experienced it. This exercise is how to prevent it, but also what to do when it is too late, when you're already emotionally overwhelmed.

Overwhelm is very much like falling into the shallow end of the pool on a warm summer day. There's no danger of drowning, all you have to do is stand up. But you must admit that you and your clothes are indeed *wet.*

What would the normal person do if he or she were to fall into that pool?

1. Get out of the pool

2. Shower off and put on dry clothing

But when we are emotionally overwhelmed, we don't always think of removing the cause of the overwhelm. When you're already past that point, you must remove your Self from the condition that is overwhelming.

Here is an example of how to perform these two important steps and what they mean.

Say you're at work and your boss gets angry with you. As you start to feel emotional overwhelm, excuse your Self to the washroom. What you are really doing by walking away for a few minutes is making a conscious choice to *change the energy*.

Getting out of the pool means changing the energy. It's a form of self-empowerment when you realize you really do have choices, and have the power to make them. Walking towards the washroom is like climbing out of the pool, out of the energy that is causing you overwhelm. It is not avoidance; it is you making a conscious choice to be in a state of calm, a state of equanimity.

What must you do next? Get out of those wet clothes, take a shower, and put on dry clothes. That means take the time to compose your Self. How?

Here's a suggestion: when in the washroom, think of one of your most sensual (of the five senses) accomplishments. Maybe the first time you held a baby, the most beautiful meadow you ever saw, the most stirring music you've ever heard.

Now, take that thought and turn it into the *feeling*. Dwell with that feeling for a few moments. As you feel those sensations, what is really happening is the "showering off and putting on dry clothes."

That means you are exercising the power of your will to choose peaceful equanimity: the quality of choosing calm when immersed in chaos. You can be surrounded by chaos without being a part of it.

As you exit the washroom, you'll notice that your feelings have completely changed, and when next you meet your boss, you are presenting to him a completely different energy, thus changing the nature of the consciousness in the interaction between the two of you.

We all fall into the shallow end from time to time. Choosing not to stay in the water requires more than wishing be dry. It is sometimes difficult to know what to do. You must *act.* Choose the calm, and choose it again. The more you apply, the more results you achieve.

Keep this exercise simple, but have it handy in case you begin to feel overwhelmed. You'll find, with time and practice, there will be much less that can cause you to experience feelings of emotional overwhelm. All because you gave your Self the power of choice.

This exercise strengthens your will to choose for your Self, to empower your Self: perception/will/reaction.

As you perceive your karmic and chakric relationships more clearly, you'll understand your part in them, and your willpower can more effectively choose a reaction that is in alignment with principles that serve your higher and greater good.

REAL CASE HISTORIES
OF CHAKRA RELATIONSHIPS

(Names and some personal aspects have been changed for anonymity.)

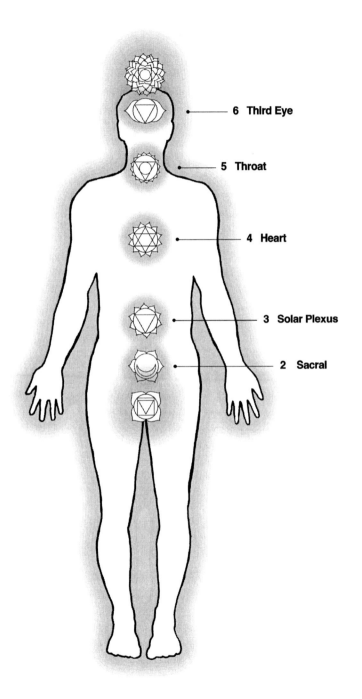

2 and 2
married psychologists

This case history was most interesting. Two brilliant people, both 2's, locked in the struggle of the lower aspects of the second chakra, which resulted in chaos and lack of direction. Both seemed eager for resolution and guidance, but neither was willing to do what was necessary to help the relationship work.

Initially they came to me for spiritual counseling. Both were practicing psychologists, yet their marriage had many difficulties, among them emotional communication and congruity of mutual goals.

The woman, Vivian, initially seemed to be very open and "seeing the big picture" as a 2 is so capable of doing. Her husband, Roger, would react to her statements with cynicism and tended to refute her positive and loving suggestions for improving their relationship.

They were locked in a deep struggle. As I guided the conversation and offered insights, she would seem positive and enthusiastic. The more enthusiastic Vivian became, the more caustic Roger became.

We had three sessions over a period of six months. When near the end of the last session, I realized that we had gotten nowhere fast. I decided to push the issue, knowing that otherwise no real progress could be made without some form of breakthrough.

As I began to push the energy of abandonment and the need for approval (two of many of the lower aspects of the second chakra), Roger got up, left the room, and did not return. I focused my attention on Vivian, feeling I had nothing to lose. Finally, she said (to my suggestions) "I can't!" I told her she could, but had it yet become worth it for her to do so? In another ten minutes, she also left the session in a hurry, and I have not seen either of them since.

There are two main problems here. First, high intellect is sometimes a real barrier to spiritual growth because the individual assumes he or she can mentally rise to any challenge and conquer it with sheer will. *Conceptual thinking and imagination are not the same thing as awareness.* It simply is not so in spirituality, because consciousness is much more than the physical mind's ability to think.

The Feminine Principle means using the power of your will to allow change into your life by yielding to your higher Self, your inner knower. It takes great strength to trust with your heart what your mind, especially if brilliant and powerful, cannot yet know. These two psychologists had an arsenal of descriptive diagnoses to label their relationship difficulties, but the terminology never addressed the key issues.

Second, one of the major lessons of the second chakra is that of faith or trust. That is, so many 2's can psychically see, through the energy of the mystic, how other people could be as whole and complete. They often make the error of assuming that is what the other person wants and desires, which is not always (ironically) the case because it leaves out the free will of the other person to choose, even if the choice is a poor one.

So often second chakra people cannot know for themselves how things will turn out - but they will know for others. The reason they cannot know is it forces them to make a commitment to their own inner faith and trust, and helps to engender self-acceptance.

This helps overcome abandonment issues and the desire

for approval that many 2's suffer from.

In this case, *both* Vivian and Roger, even though Ph.D. trained psychologists, suffered from these lower aspects, and neither were willing to take the leap of faith necessary to build a strong sense of inner acceptance.

The law of cause and effect is surely at work here. Unless one of them changes, nothing in the relationship will change. If Vivian walks out of the room saying "I can't," then she can't, until she trusts that she can.

I knew by the third session that nothing was going to change unless I pushed it. It is a risk I took as a spiritual counselor because they were deadlocked.

Perhaps, in time, Vivian and Roger will see their mutual goals as positive and will seek a more harmonious relationship. Imagine bringing that type of mirror into your life: someone who is a pretty accurate reflection of you in the same chakra!

4-2 and 3
a mother and her brilliant son

Beth is a 4-2 and Christopher, her son, is a 3. As a parent, Beth was concerned about Christopher's powerful third chakra expression. He is brilliant and alert, and she is a kind and loving mother. She sought counseling to know how best to raise Christopher, given his exceptionally strong personality.

The irony of life is that we can possess opposite desirable characteristics of a given chakra simultaneously. In the case of the third chakra, a person can voraciously consume education for material gain all in the name of Self, but the same person can ardently avoid making any emotional decisions that requires them to feel the qualitative properties related to the emotion.

In this case, Beth is a mother of three children with Christopher the middle child, age eleven. Being a 3, Christopher is brilliant and hungry for life's experiences. Medical doctors have classified him as ADHD (I think many of us would have been classified as such if the same practices in medicine and psychology were in effect when we were kids) and recommended a program of drugs. Wisely, Beth declined and is instead considering how best to help Christopher with the possibility of home schooling.

I say wisely because she has given much thought to the positive and negative effects of long-term mood-altering drugs and knew of the problem of weaning children off them. In other words, the drugs do help to a degree, but they only biochemically assist the individual, which does not address the root cause of the problem. (To me, a person is much more than biochemical or physical. One must include the mental, emotional and spiritual components when treating for any illness or condition. Therefore, any program of such drugs should include therapy and spiritual counseling/healing work as well.)

In the movie "Good Will Hunting," the star, played by Matt Damon, had a genius mentality and was able to conceptualize and mentalize so well that he intimidated his peers. The problem was that all his knowledge was not based on *experience*, and as a result there was no emotional grounding in his sense Self. He could mentally go there, but had no real sense of his true power, uniqueness, or inner truth.

Sometimes 3's have a voracious appetite for the accumulation of education, money, power, the "essence of the thing itself," etc. But as the fruit comes forth when it is ready, all things have their own time to mature. Out-of-balance 3's can continually seek more personal challenges without ever really addressing the fundamental challenge to their chakra dominance: to make emotional decisions related to Self. That is, the greatest fear of 3's is that they really are that powerful. It is one of the facets of the third chakra they came to experience. But the 3 comes to learn how to make qualitative decisions based on uniqueness, and like the wise king, there must be some experience that leads to the wise use of power.

Imagine how many people could be manipulated by a powerful 3 until that person learns to control his power. Or how many relationships a 3 might go through before understanding what personal power means and how it affects the lives of others. Or how the 3 could be the eternal student, always looking for greater challenges, but each challenge only stimulates the 3 for more accumulation of education, or power, money, material gain, etc.

What type of person would Christopher bring into his

life to reflect back to him the balance he seeks? Is the heart chakra (4) a good combination for a strong 3?

Beth, because she is a 4-2, represents the quality of what love is. The reciprocity between her and Christopher, energetically, is that she will show him what love is (95% percent of which is energetic, meaning at all times, especially because parent/child karma is the strongest karma there is). She loves and accepts him unconditionally, and his higher Self is aware of the purity the fourth chakra represents through her past lives of dharma. Her affect on him is acceptance, calming, nurturing, a place for him to just "be" instead of being concerned that he is a strong mentalized projection of his imagined Self.

Christopher, through his third chakra, will reflect back to her how to individuate her power, how to be strong in her opinions, even though you can imagine it is emotionally challenging for a parent to raise such a child. Remember that this works best when each person is living to his or her highest potential (right action, dharma), and that doing so represents the highest possibility that the other person could benefit by then making right decisions. Sometimes children do not yet understand what the parent does. So, it falls to the parents to do the best they can.

Prayer and meditation are always great ways to empower one's Self and to spiritually evolve out of the dilemmas in life caused through chakra dominance and karma. If there is a measure of karma in the relationship (again, parent/child being the strongest karma), spiritual practices always help to relieve the karma.

Bear in mind that some karma lasts a very long time, and spiritual practices can help to reduce that time, but sometimes people need their lessons and infirmities in order to evolve. This is why some people do not heal immediately. It is not because the prayers and the spiritual healing do not work, it is because the karma is based on the illusion of separation from the Oneness, and each of us must work to reduce our own karma in divine timing. As we each evolve, the karma dissipates.

As their relationship matures, there is always the possibility that no matter what Beth does as a mother, her son is going to do what he will. However, the only way Beth can truly be of service to her son is to live in the higher aspect of her fourth chakra. By living her life well, she fully represents her potential as a 4; to represent the quality of what love is. It is the relationship that she and Christopher chose in this lifetime. How better could he heal than to have a parent who represents love and healing, and is doing everything she can to help him?

If you ask, "What about her other two children, one older and one younger than Christopher? How can she best raise them?"

The answer is the same: by living in the higher aspects of her given dominant chakra and avoiding the choices that exhibit lower chakra aspects, Beth energetically represents the highest and greatest possibility to which her children can evolve, because she has chosen to do so.

3 and 5
lovers reincarnated

This is a fascinating story that originated from one of my workshops on karma and reincarnation. I had been teaching these workshops for years. The general protocol is a one-hour lecture, followed by a pertinent past-life evaluation for the attendees.

A man and woman were sitting next to each other in the workshop. I told them both that there was a lot of love flowing and flowering between them and I asked if they knew each other.

The woman, Sharon, replied that she is a patient of his; that Tom is a naturopathic doctor. I told them that they were married in a past life, that he had died in her arms, and that there was a very strong bond between them that was meant to be explored in this lifetime.

I also told Tom that he was bitten by some form of insect carrying a deadly infection and that there is a birthmark on the back of his neck in this lifetime from the bite in that previous life. Upon examination, there is such a mark on his neck. Interesting that the birthmark in this lifetime would be in the location of his dominant fifth chakra.

Then I jokingly added that I was an ordained Reverend and performed marriage ceremonies. They blanched a bit at my directness, but I could clearly see the loving, karmic relationship between them and the unfolding of a new one.

As it turned out, Sharon, who is a 3, did express an interest in Tom, who is a 5. Under healing protocol and ethics, Tom must stop treating Sharon clinically for at least six months before they could date each other. Sharon noticed some reticence on Tom's part, partly because as a 5 he had trouble grounding.

I advised her to think of the word "ground" when speaking with him, to pull him back down into his body. Over a period of time, Sharon expressed disappointment to me that Tom simply was not responding to this intense energy of romantic partnership, which she so deeply felt.

As it turns out, Tom announced he developed a relationship with someone else and that he was moving to another town to set up a new practice. This made Sharon very distraught, but I later found out that Sharon had not done as I advised.

She did that very lower aspect of third chakra things; she procrastinated telling Tom how she really felt about him. Not having anything concrete to go on, he developed another relationship.

This brought up two points:

First, Sharon procrastinated against her emotional choices and acts of will based on her emotions; a fundamental error and cause of much suffering for third chakra people.

Second, *men do not take hints*. (Be direct with your partner; don't make him guess your intentions.)

In retrospect, Tom should have been more grounded and listened clearly to what I told him in the workshop. He tended to be very mentally busy, and when 5's do that too much they become emotionally unavailable.

I doubt the startup of his new practice will be successful, because he moved for all the wrong reasons. I also suspect that he will move back to the town where Sharon lives, and will eventually pick up the relationship with her again.

Sharon should not have procrastinated and should have told her true feelings. One of the things a 3 can do well is procrastinate, especially away from emotional decisions.

The worst thing that could have happened is that he could have not shared the same romantic feelings with her. But if she had leveled with him, as a third chakra person can, she would have known the answer.

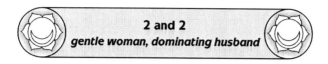

2 and 2
gentle woman, dominating husband

Here is one that I see from time to time, though not always in this particular chakra set relationship. Susan is a woman who has been in the healthcare field her entire adult life. Gentle and compassionate, she suffers as some 2's can, quietly and with moderate amounts of despair. Hopelessness and emotional overwhelm are sometimes the worst part of the dilemmas that face a 2 from the lower aspect.

The lower aspect of the second chakra can cause one to feel there are no alternatives, when the true strength of that chakra is infinite alternatives. This is ironic, but true, as is the case for all the chakras. It doesn't seem to make sense, but there it is. It is also ironic that were issues not emotional, but say, financial, we would know much more about how to address them. But when issues are emotional, we seem to lack the skills to cope with the hardships they present.

Susan's husband, Brad, is a very successful, hard-working man who has, through the years, helped accumulate money and material things to make a comfortable life for the couple. However, he always seems to be working hard on the next project, not satisfied that enough is enough.

One of the lower aspects of the second chakra is "Nothing I do is ever good enough." Some interpret this as ever-striving for the accumulation of material goods and when reaching a plateau, starting yet another endeavor. This can lead to instability in a relationship, because Brad is always working, and is in that rationalization trap of "It is the work I'm doing that is providing the means for our lifestyle." And yet, so much time can slip by before one realizes that the important thing is the relationship itself, not the accumulation of comforts that surround it.

So many women I've counseled would settle for a little less material comfort and more quality time with their partners. As it is, Susan's life is not settling into a groove because Brad is always creating more material income, moving their residence. Do you think there is good emotional communication going on here?

What should Susan do? Create a stronger identity of herself? Better healthy emotional boundaries?

One of the greatest things a 2 can do is to gain from regular inspiration. Everyone has something that inspires them, whether it is watching a sunset, attending musical concerts, admiring great art, etc.

The inspiration sparks the infinite creativity that the second chakra represents. It reminds the 2 there are so many alternatives, so many options, so much to live for. It would otherwise become quite overwhelming to face such infinite alternatives, but in metaphysics, your strength is your weakness and your weakness is your strength. The fact that Susan felt powerless to speak to Brad about her own desires came from the lack of confidence in her own creative abilities. An illusion to be sure, but a very effective one that caused her to feel the quiet desperation in her relationship.

Inspiration, when done regularly, offers two hidden benefits: you begin to have a sense of your own identity because you get more perspective on your life; and you begin to feel more of your integrity because you know more of what you will and will not accept.

If you think about it, here she is surrounded by all the appointments of material gain and material stability, but is starving for emotional nurturing. Even so, she had been a nurse in the healthcare field for years, offering loving compassion and care to the infirm.

Why would she attract another 2 like Brad, who ostensibly is a good man, working hard to provide for his partner, and yet still be in "violent agreement" with him? That is another way of saying he's providing in the way he thinks he can and must, but the fundamental elements of a great relationship are missing. The formula for providing in such a way seems great on paper, but in practice something is still missing. What is it? What is the reflection that Susan has brought into her life?

The second chakra is the visceral chakra, more connected to the five senses than any other chakra. It is also the chakra of infinite creativity and possibilities. Most who are second dominant externalize their gifts by caring for others in some way. Brad is the provider, and Susan is the caregiver. But what happens when a caregiver asks for nothing in return? Should Susan just expect Brad to know?

One of the great strengths of the second chakra is called "the energy of the mystic." It means there is an inherent psychic ability to see others as how they could be as whole and complete. We all have it, but it is particularly strong in 2's. If you will recall, the mind capitulates to the strength of the consciousness flowing through a given dominant chakra, so in this case the mind is always assuming it should be creating for others. But what is missing is the self-acceptance, the commitment one must make to their own "sweetness" (a Buddhist term, meaning that which is already perfect within you).

In other words, you must first accept your Self as whole and complete, that what you do is good enough, that you avoid self-criticism and self-destructive tendencies. The 2 can see others as whole and complete and expects the others would naturally desire it as well. But as I said, we live in a world of irony. What might make perfect sense to one person may never materialize in another.

I have counseled many women who "saw" how their partner could be as whole and complete, but the partner was not ready, willing, or able to do so. You must be willing to recognize, if you are a 2, that you can indeed have the correct intuitive answer for someone in a relationship, that you really do see accurately how they could be as whole and complete.

It is essential to realize that the other person also has a free will, independent of yours, to choose as they will, even if it is a poor choice.

In the case of Susan and Brad, both were hard-working individuals in an emotionally starved relationship. If Susan spends time in inspiration and heads in the direction her inner knower provides through increased perspective, she can place the value on her relationship with Brad where it is most needed, in emotional closeness. If Brad is unwilling to meet her halfway, then the problem remains.

The difference between compromise and settling is that when a couple compromise, they are willing to meet each other halfway. When one of the couple settles, she is giving away part of her integrity in order to make peace.

Do you suppose Susan is settling by being quiet to maintain the illusion of harmony in the relationship? Unfortunately, some people suffer a very long time until they change the energy of the relationship, sometimes when it is too late.

Regular inspiration, emotional communication, and healthy emotional boundaries would be of great help, but also Susan must make that commitment to her own self-worth, her sacred value to herself as a being equal to Brad or anyone else.

There is an old saying: "You get in life what you settle for."

What are *you* willing to settle for? Is it worth it for you to communicate to your partner? Are you settling? Are you placing a value on your Self? When does the time come when you've suffered enough? I've a rather dark humor when I've told my students, "They've stopped giving out medals for how long you can suffer and hold onto pain."

One other major factor to consider in the lower aspect of the 2 is the use of guilt. Guilt, like fear, is a wonderful/terrible motivator. It does not require a shred of truth to be effective, and 2's are particularly susceptible to guilt as a manipulating device. In fact, once you've hooked a 2 on guilt, it requires very little thereafter to continue the manipulation. These types of associations can last for years.

Do you suspect that Susan would feel guilty, imprisoned by her guilt, for saying anything to Brad because when she looked around at all her material surroundings (most provided by Brad) she could find no error or problem? That maybe she should just keep her mouth shut? How many times have we seen people with many material luxuries who have become miserable because they are spiritually unfulfilled? What if Susan feels guilty, and Brad is not knowingly applying any guilt but providing (in his own mind) the best for her that he can? Would that not be an emotional tragedy?

The inspiration I spoke of earlier is also a key way to help awaken your higher sense-perceptions. If Susan were to apply more inspiration, to awaken her higher sense-perceptions, she would invariably see her husband as he truly is. The same would be true for Brad, if he were to spend time in inspiration and contemplative thinking.

So, a 2 attracted another visceral, life-loving 2 in an emotional relationship for the possibility of spiritual growth. The possibility is always there, but sometimes we don't see it as an opportunity, but rather as a trap. If you realize that the second chakra represents infinite creativity, then the very thing that made you weak can once again make you strong. In other words, if you turn the emotional overwhelm from infinite possibilities into the realization of your identity and integrity through inspiration and fierce love of your 'sweetness', you begin to live in the higher aspect of the second chakra.

What should Brad do? So many men I've counseled, like Brad, see themselves as hard-working providers, yet their relationships are unfulfilled. The first and most important step, for many men, is to become better emotional communicators.

Many women are not necessarily looking for the answer as much as they are looking for the recognition that there can be better and deeper emotional involvement with their partners. It comes from each person as an emotional vulnerability. Many men look at this as a form of weakness; that deeper emotional communication is not manly.

Men, if you're reading this, you can get more emotional frequent flyer mileage with a woman by noticing and communicating the nuances and subtleties of your relationship with her, because most women are psychically tuned into such cues.

Does that mean you need to be a "sensitive man?" Certainly not. In true metaphysics, it means you are vulnerable to your Self, to your capacity to grow as a spiritual being having a physical existence. Doing so naturally includes the awakening of your higher sense-perceptions.

Many, many more women are aware of their higher sense-perceptions than men. In fact, women are hard-wired more than men to be balanced in the left and right hemispheres of their brains. Across the corpus calossum, a bony plate that separates the left and right hemispheres of the brain, there is a bundle of nerve fibers that connects both hemispheres. In a man, the bundle of nerves is the thickness of a human hair (0.003 inches). In a woman, the bundle of nerves is the thickness of a pencil. You do the math.

This is partly why I have so many more women students and workshop participants (about 90% women) than men.

Men - to be vulnerable means to trust your feelings, even beyond your fine logical capabilities. Your higher sense-perceptions are as powerful as a woman's, but culturally repressed. Remember, the smallest feeling is greater than the greatest thought.

Do you suppose Brad stops for a moment to reflect what he is feeling for Susan? Do you suppose he also pauses to reflect on how she might be feeling? Perhaps by Susan not communicating her true feelings, he is genuinely unaware that there is a problem that has been brewing for years. This is why some men are quite in the dark when their partner decides a drastic change is needed in the relationship.

I also suspect that Brad, like some second chakra men, is looking to be "rescued" by his loving and gentle partner, Susan. Watch the movie "What Women Want" with actor Mel Gibson. In the end, it did not matter that he could read women's minds. What he desired was to be rescued from himself through the love of Helen Hunt's character.

Is that a sign of weakness? Did he think she would complete him? No, he desired deep and fulfilling love and knew he must bring balance into his life through the reflection of a partner who was already individually powerful and did not need him, but desired and loved him. She reflected back to him his own vulnerability to surrender to infinite possibilities.

Instead of wanting to know and control the future, evolved 2's must trust and have faith in themselves that the alternatives they seek really are there, even if there is no physical evidence to support it. Mel could no longer read Helen's mind, because he did not need to. He surrendered to his own inner preciousness, through faith. And only after surrender can a person evolve.

It's like an epiphany. If you knew what an epiphany was, would it be an epiphany? No, of course not. It is the surrender to the unknown, through faith, that true evolution of consciousness comes about. One cannot think their way into an evolved consciousness, but rather surrender to the higher, more eloquent aspects of the Self that exist in the continuum of the Oneness, where there is no separation and no illusion.

These are life issues not meant to be overcome in a weekend. Yielding to your inner faith and trust is sometimes very difficult, when all we want to do is try to control the outcome. It is better to guide the outcome through faith, than to try to control it with your mind.

Remember, life is about the development of your character, not about the accumulation of accomplishments and material things. The real value you add to a relationship is the character you bring to it through your own self-development.

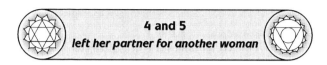

4 and 5
left her partner for another woman

Here is a case history of two women in a partnership that had lasted many years, until one day Teresa (5) told Allison (4) that it was over and that she was leaving her for another woman.

It does not seem likely that Allison had even considered this was a possibility, as their relationship had gone beyond eighteen years and there was no real sign of trouble. What, she thought, could possibly bring the whole sky crashing down around her like this?

Unwittingly, 4's can be overwhelming in their desire to love and protect those around them. Often, the energy that is externalized is called "the preserver and the conserver." The 4 seeks to preserve that which is pure in a person and/or the relationship: in this case, with Teresa, a fifth chakra woman.

I found Teresa to be the quintessential 5, very much the communicator and working diligently on being grounded. Over the years, I'd counseled both of them from time to time on life issues, and in their relationship to each other.

The fact that Teresa would leave the relationship was devastating to Allison. It shows how the power of two wills can be at odds when the basis of the relationship seems to be intact.

Allison's world fell apart and she became emotionally overwhelmed and distraught. She could not perceive where anything could possibly be wrong or how the strings of their beautiful relationship could come undone in such a manner. Allison could not understand what she did "wrong" or how Teresa could leave their relationship for another.

What was Allison doing that was unfulfilling for Teresa? Was it Allison's fault? When relationships break up like this, there are usually seeds of separation that have sprouted long before the actual break-up occurs.

I suspect in this case that Allison, by her loving nature, was unwittingly smothering, which is something you cannot do to a fifth chakra dominant person. It is hard enough for the 5 to even try to stay grounded on the earth plane, much less be involved in the avalanche of love that pours forth from an empowered 4.

Allison is kind and loving, gentle and compassionate; composed of all the good qualities one would expect to find in a 4. But I think Teresa was feeling constrained by that love, not free as she would like to be within that love. Teresa was perhaps also enacting that part of the 5 personality that becomes the hermit, then externalizes again in another group of people (or in this case with another person). Even that's not as good an explanation as: fifth chakra people can only be grounded for so long, unless they are really spiritually developed, the smothering was probably something that was happening on a fairly regular basis.

What should Allison do? Teresa left, moved all her belongings out, and is now living with (and in love) with another woman. One thing this reminds us of is that we have our own free will to choose, but we must remember that everyone else has a free will to choose as well, even (and especially) if it makes no sense to us. This is so very difficult for Allison, because of her kind and gentle nature. The hurt she feels is equally profound to her ability to give such great love.

I've counseled many people over the years whose most pressing question to me was "Why?" Without the benefit of the other person's communication, many people have been left in the metaphorical dark to make assumptions and conclusions on their own, and this is most difficult when we are seeking closure in emotional relationships.

Yes, Teresa's fifth chakra would be helping and reflecting back to Allison to articulate what she could not otherwise say, and even to increase Allison's comprehension of the emotional communication between the two. How do you suppose Allison would have reacted if Teresa were to tell her that she was emotionally smothering her? Be in shock? What if Teresa explained it carefully? Does that mean Allison would understand? No, in this case she does not.

Remember, that the fifth chakra person can explain very carefully and with great articulation, but that does not mean others are ready to understand. The 5 has to know when to let go, when no understanding may yet take place. Remember, you cannot *make* someone else understand you. Understanding comes from within, from being open to the possibility that understanding could take place. Even then, it does not mean that it will.

If you will also recall that life is about the development of one's character, then how do you suppose it would help someone to move on with their life if they did not have a full understanding? It is similar to meditation. Meditation is not the place you arrive at, it is the *effort* of balancing mind/heart, soul/body, yin/yang that defines the meditation. It is the effort to *maintain balance* that defines your character, not the balance itself.

As a 4, Allison may spend years trying to understand the lesson she learned with a relationship with fifth chakra Teresa, but the real lesson is in her efforts to understand, not the understanding itself. Therefore, a "why" may be a long time coming, but it is better to continue to make the effort to achieve balance than to capitulate into an emotional depression where no balance is possible. Easy to say, hard to do.

Would you say that if Allison has not learned this lesson, that she may attract yet another person into her life who will reflect back to her lessons in meaning, comprehension, and understanding?

Teresa may find what she's looking for in a new relationship, but she did spend a great many years in this one. Sometimes it's hard to know when you've reached that point in a relationship where it's time to end it. Most counselors, including me, attempt to help preserve the relationship and find ways to achieve mutual goals and desires.

But one only has to look at the divorce rate to know that many people are making these difficult choices not to stay in the relationship. Relationships take effort and commitment. Perhaps, in this case, Allison and Teresa are better served by moving on. The gurus have a saying: "In the end, it is between you and God."

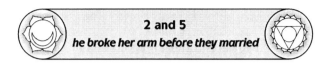

2 and 5
he broke her arm before they married

A difficult story to tell, because there is much suffering sprinkled in an otherwise delightful life. A woman, Fay (2), was to marry, for the first time, a man I'll call Xavier (5). Three weeks before their marriage date, they were in a heated argument. Xavier became so angry, he broke Fay's arm. Yet, three weeks later she still married him. Why?

Perhaps she was used to some form of abuse for many years, and this was but one step on a many-tiered platform of self-discovery, where the second chakra person does not change until they've suffered enough. Louise Hay said: "Sometimes the bowl of our love is scoured out by deep pain so that we can know great love." Some 2's, because the second chakra is the most connected to our five senses, must experience through those five senses deeply so that they have the experience of the sensation, even though it be great pain.

Why such difficult lessons exist is hard to fathom. Any reasonable person would have advised her not to marry the man: perhaps he would do something even worse in the future. In fact, that is what happened.

After she had a child who was now two, Fay was again pregnant. Xavier and Fay argued, and the result was he struck her so hard it permanently put her jaw out of position. The trauma threatened the life of the child to the extent Fay had to go to the hospital in fear of losing the baby. The baby was ok, and was later born normally. But can you imagine being either of those children, whether in utero or growing up, in such a condition of contention and strife?

It took Fay another five years before she finally ended the relationship. Xavier was a successful businessman, but had no real emotional availability to his wife and family. Being a 5, Xavier was "out of body" most of the time, always in his head, which made him very emotionally unavailable. He externalized his ungroundedness and emotional unavailability through violence, and Fay was the receptor, perhaps because of self-esteem, perhaps because her second chakra accurately saw the good in this man, and she hoped that his inherent goodness would surface someday. It did not, but imagine the courage this woman had, to take the tremendous abuse that Xavier would give her, and yet remain.

Sometimes when we are challenged emotionally, we don't know what to do or how to respond as well as if the situation were about finances, or building a house. It seems practicality and reasonableness disappear in times of great emotional stress, leaving us without an escape to end our suffering.

What would the average person have advised Fay? To get out at the first sign of abuse? I would have. But we are not living the life of that individual. As Joseph Campbell says: "We each pick our own entrance into the dark forest of our shadow selves." Fay, in this case, stayed in a relationship where the lesson would be hard to fathom. What would the reciprocity be? What would Xavier be reflecting back to her? And from Fay to Xavier?

It has been said that the only way you can really change others is to change your Self. That if you wish to make a positive impact on the world, you live your life as well as you can. It makes sense, according to the 95% rule.

Xavier is an ungrounded man, in search of his identity. The greatest fear of a 5 is that no one will ever know him for who he really is. This can externalize through the fifth chakra dominance in a variety of ways. In Xavier's case, he would beat Fay to make himself "right." That in part, is why Xavier is really a 5/3 (fifth chakra dominant, with a reference to his third chakra). Meaning, if he is first ungrounded in the fifth chakra, he could also suffer in the third, giving way to the need to be right, to anger, and to taking things personally.

And if you look at the numbers, chakras 5 and 3 are male (masculine energy, or yang) chakras. That's a lot of assertive energy, especially if ungrounded.

Fay is second chakra. She is reflecting passion to Xavier; passion for life, for love, for the senses. So often, when a 5 and a 2 get together, the possibilities are very good because the 5 articulates for the 2 what the 2 has difficulty getting into effect. In other words, 2's are the visionaries, but sometimes cannot articulate or explain their vision.

The 2 helps to ground the 5 in the third dimension of the physical senses. The 2 can be lusty about life; that includes everything from sex and sensuality to the preciousness of life itself. Fay offered to Xavier an abandoned woman, who was looking to invest all of her love in him to help him heal his emotional ungroundedness. Her dominant second chakra knew, on some level, what to do to help him, but so many years went by and he would not change, while the emotional scars kept piling up in Fay's life's experiences.

I have seen cases where an abused woman leaves the abusive relationship, but then cannot successfully have a relationship with a man who is non-abusive. She ends the relationship in order to find another abusive man. It is supremely difficult to trust, once your trust has been shattered. It is also supremely necessary to do just that, so that you do not end up in another relationship that is the same as the one you just left.

The reason to trust is that it nurtures your own

preciousness, your own ability to bring a reflection back to you that is a sign of your self-respect and the ferocity by which you are willing to love your Self and hence bring the possibility of great love into your life.

Is it possible? You bet it is!! How do you do it? One way is for Fay to associate with like-minded women; those who represent an uplifting and outgoing attitude toward life. Another is for her to join her local church or temple, and to make strong spiritual connections with people who are devoted to God and to perfecting their lives. Living among that energy definitely has an effect on a person.

The more Fay learns to trust and nurture her true feelings, the less abandonment or desire for approval she'll externalize. The more fiercely she loves and trusts herself, the less she will need others to validate her existence.

What about Xavier? Once Fay leaves him, there is his life, and the shared life of the children. What can Xavier do to ground himself and to relieve the karma he has created by his violence with Fay?

Many fifth chakra persons are teacher/communicators and seek explanations for the manner in which the universe unfolds. Perhaps bringing a true spiritual teacher into his life would help, someone authentic in metaphysical/spiritual awareness who could help guide his search for meaning and comprehension, as so many 5's do in a lifetime.

He could also read books on the subject, but reading alone would never be enough. If willing, he could join groups where he can learn different ways to communicate his frustrations and anger, and perhaps most importantly take up yoga, spiritual practices, or meditative techniques to help him be more grounded and focused.

5 and 5
sisters in a past life
find each other again

This case also came from one of my workshops on karma and reincarnation. Two women in attendance had been friends for five years. I told them that they had been sisters in a past life in Lucern, Switzerland in the 15th century. I went on to tell each of them details about that lifetime and how it related to this one.

I then asked them to say a little about themselves. The first one, Marlee, said that she visited Lucern, Switzerland some fifteen years ago. The second one, Vickie, said that she visited Lucern, Switzerland, ten years ago.

It had been a happy lifetime for them, as sisters, in a farming community in the 15th century. They had contracted, karmically, to meet once again. It was obvious from meeting them that not only were they both 5's, but they were also both very evolved into the higher aspects. They did not suffer so much from the ungroundedness, mentalisms and emotional unavailability that so often accompany fifth chakra personalities as they are developing.

What had actually happened is a "cellular memory," a geographical trigger point where, in different years of their present lives they each set foot on the same land they lived on together in a past life, not consciously knowing of each other's existence in this lifetime. This triggering set about the course of events, which were to follow (their inner guidance like radar), so they could "find" each other on the planet and re-connect as sisters in this lifetime, though this time biologically unrelated.

You'll find from time to time that familial and intimate relationships will continue in future lifetimes, sometimes because the karma was so good. Not all karma is bad, but rather "bad" and "good" karma is still karma; attachment to one's actions rooted in the illusion of separation from the Oneness.

Vickie and Marlee are both very much fifth chakra persons, teachers by profession. In fact, I learned that their posting in the school system was to teach the teachers. Having had a loving, pastoral life centuries ago could have really grounded them to come in this lifetime as 5's. The result is that they would very quickly aspire and achieve the higher aspects of the fifth chakra.

Remember, though you may be a 5, that does not mean you must physically teach. The 95% that is energy helps to heal comprehension and understanding in the world, even if you are just mounting tires on cars all day. It is the quality of who you are and what you represent as a soul incarnate, not your profession, which defines you.

Perhaps to their credit, 5's also engender an amount of telepathy, so maybe it was easier for these women to end up in California and find each other again, 500 years later. An interesting note about fifth chakra telepaths is that the ability crosses kingdoms, as well, into the elemental, plant, and animal kingdoms. I've seen several 5's have great pets, become veterinarians, open plant and flower shops, become essential oil practitioners, and more.

3 and 3
clash of the Titans

I know a woman, Uma, who is married to a man, Peter, and they both are 3's. They have children, and Uma is a very good mother to them. Peter seems to do a considerable amount of traveling, which in itself may be part of what can keep the marriage going.

Perhaps if Uma and Peter were in a relationship where they saw each other all the time there would be much more contention. The third chakra, when unchecked, can be an extreme taskmaster, as the search for truth and the essence (the bottom line) can intensify all their encounters, create power struggles and egoic manipulation.

As you may know from the lower aspects, a person can "need to be right." Because her personality was so strong, Uma could engage and take over social and group settings and move the energy in her favor in a manipulative manner. This would cause power struggles and contention and tend to distract groups from their original purpose. Part of this was a healthy reality check because 3's do bring a higher level of truth to their encounters, if they themselves are living in the higher aspect.

Uma seeks contention because at the base of her third chakra is the strong desire to know the truth of things. It has externalized to a blunt and sometimes abrasive personality, which is neither good nor bad, though it does strain many of her relationships. When faced with such true internal power, many 3's lament that they've no peers, no equals with whom they can associate. And they are partly right.

So the possibility for great conflict is always there for

Uma because she seeks out people and groups who will be the reflection of her desire to know what power is. Those groups of people will always appear, because the Uma's consciousness is constantly creating the unfolding scenario of circumstances whereby she can overcome her illusions, but also experience the possibility of right use of her personal power.

Uma's husband, Peter, is also a 3 but is more inwardly calm and stable, and hence tends to ameliorate any possible contention between the two of them by not turning Uma's power issues into a conflagration of egos.

This is a case where even though both parties in the relationship are 3's, there is enough difference between them that power struggles do not seem to be an issue. Also, when 3's align in harmony, there can be great strides in the ability to ultimately lead very spiritual lives and give truth to the world.

2 and Various
a reverse chaotic manipulator

A woman I'll call Marcia '2' ran a large metaphysical bookstore. This is an interesting story because she related to each of her employees in the same manner even though they were of various chakra dominances.

Reverse chaotic manipulators use the power of their second chakra in its *lower* aspect to keep people off-guard and off-balance. The reason for this is that they never have to become responsible for their own stuff if everyone around them is always put on the defensive. It's a way of avoiding certain emotional responsibilities and exerting control.

Who would come in contact with this person? The staff, the psychics who work for Marcia, even the public. Here is a central figure who, by her profession, is supposed to assist people to their self-empowerment through metaphysical means, and yet is inured deeply in her own chaos to the point where she must keep all around her at bay.

Another irony? Real life is better than the soap operas. People who worked for her who quit did so for a variety of reasons, but not until they told Marcia their true feelings about her. I would like to think the reason they did that was noble: to help Marcia realize that her reverse chaotic manipulation was most destructive to her business, her employees, and patrons, but mostly to herself.

Second chakra people can become very self-destructive when the perfect psychic image they accurately perceive on the higher levels of themselves does not match what their minds tell them they *should* have achieved. Again, this is the grand illusion: the difference between the physical mind assuming it is in control and the higher, true reality of the Self coming through the chakra system, with one chakra being more emphasized than the others.

In this case, there may be desperation to be in control. It makes sense, because of the infinitely creative aspect of the second chakra; the physical mind capitulates and tries to control in the physical plane what is happening in a continuum on higher planes of existence.

Remember the greatest fear of the second chakra? The fear that one cannot create anything greater than that which came before. So, perhaps Marcia was responding to this fundamental fear by playing out an elaborate game of control, where everyone but she would be off-balance, and she could be the one in control, even without seeming to be. That's pretty good.

Ultimately, schemes like this are meant to self-destruct and fall apart in the light of new awareness. Another irony is working in a place where seekers are looking for tools for their enlightenment, their emancipation from the illusion of separation - and the owner may not realize that by her own actions she is creating the healing she herself is looking for (by the Law of Reciprocity).

Inviting such different people into the store in the capacity of employees and patrons guaranteed a mix of various levels of spiritual evolution. Marcia was sitting in an environment where the intention is light and the fulfillment of the soul: psychics working there daily, counseling and exhorting patrons to live in a higher purpose; authors doing signings for books to help heal the human condition of suffering and infirmity; the books themselves - everything from astrology to Zen Buddhism, devoted to uncovering the mystery of our true existence.

Where better to seek healing than to own such an establishment? It guarantees that Marcia would bring in the very people who would reflect back to her the means to accomplish her own healing, even though she (in her lower aspect) assumed she was the one in control. Sometimes, the universe drags you kicking and screaming into your own bliss.

In metaphysics there are elegant machinations of this universe unfolding that are quite beyond the workings of our minds, but within the grasp of our hearts. This is why we yearn with our hearts for what our physical minds cannot yet know. Our feelings transcend time and space. Physical thinking does not.

4 and 3
the genius and the earth mother

Reese is a fourth chakra man, certainly a genius by my standards. His partner, Dominique, is a 3 and is the epitome of the Earth Mother (grounded, preserver of life, defender of the innocent, versed in the healing arts, especially massage).

Reese has been involved in leading-edge technology most of his life, developing gee-whiz gadgets that are far beyond the comprehension of most people. He is also a 4, so what happens when you mix a person who is here to be the quality of what love is with a genius mentality?

Well, the fourth chakra person comes to learn how to communicate emotionally, but what if you're so brilliant most people cannot understand you, and if you are so empathic, you deeply feel the feelings of others, but you hold most of it in? You'd have a person who is rather like a pressure cooker, who externalizes his deep love for the world in the devices he makes.

However, there is no real intimate communication there, and that is what the fourth chakra person comes to learn. He, in the past, had a tendency to absorb himself in his work: work that benefits the world yet does not reveal the true tenderness in his heart to a possible beloved. Instead, he would work harder and eventually become self-destructive, as there was no outlet for his emotions through the reflection of another person.

As he hit his own emotional bottom, having bouts with mild to medium forms of depression that can come through the fourth chakra, Reese decided to quit the job he had designing high-end devices to increase human potential. He moved back to the city of his roots, and there he found Dominique, the metaphysical mama, earth lady, and shaman. She quietly knew his pain and gave him comfort, support, and a place to lay his weary heart.

It did not matter that he could not explain in multi-syllables the great ideas he had for the world; she was already way ahead of him because she had developed her third chakra in the manner most commensurate: truly spiritual but not religious. She saw Reese as he was, a harmless beautiful man whose heart was intent on healing this world through his science, and when he realized that she truly saw him, he at last knew a measure of peace in his life.

He was able to reflect God back to him in the person of Dominique with the third chakra dominance. She was strong enough in her character and moral/ethical convictions to handle his genius in a way that bypassed his intellect and went straight to his heart.

Here is a case where some would say the difference in intelligence could be a factor, yet these two souls effortlessly bypassed it to the reality of their love for each other.

Dominique's third chakra, in a way, protected the innocence of Reese, allowing him a space to be without being put upon by others. Inherently, everyone wants a piece of a fourth chakra person because they emanate the quality of purity in their hearts from past lifetimes lived well in dharma. Since we all take psychic relationships to each other, and since 4's are only 1 in 25, we are naturally attracted to people with fourth chakra dominance. If you observe Reese, a genius with a harmless heart, it is easy to see how he might become manipulated and set upon by others who only want him for what he can do for them.

Dominique brought a brilliant but caring man into her life. She no longer was trying to do it alone, to remain strong, or to try to be "right." When Reese came into her life, she was a single mom with a little girl. She had been determined to do it on her own.

Dominique realized she could be strong in her own right and still bring in her balance: the profoundly deep well of love that the fourth chakra represents. She found a man who could love her deeply, without saying a word, without needing to demonstrate his intelligence. She saw his harmlessness and his innocence, and a great relationship developed.

When I've interacted with Reese, I have always been very careful of his time and energy; always respectful of his limits. So many people in his life have misunderstood him, not realizing the intensely gentle man that he is. Without healthy emotional boundaries, it is easy to see how Reese could eventually overwork himself and become self-destructive.

When Dominique came into his life, she helped to protect him, as the third chakra person (in their higher aspect) will protect those who cannot protect themselves. Reese loves her unconditionally, and their relationship has flourished.

Dominique's third chakra dominance is reflecting back truth, uniqueness, and power, the three main energies related to the third chakra. Her individuation of the truth is helping Reese to find his, and to ultimately establish for himself the healthy emotional boundaries that he lacked. Being so pure in his heart, perhaps he felt there would be no one in the world who would not take advantage of him.

You know, even monasteries have great, big wooden doors on them. Even though the monks are harmless, they recognize there are other people in the world who are not harmless. It's OK to be a monk and to know Kung Fu. It helps, by having healthy emotional boundaries, to maintain the integrity of your beingness in this world.

What Reese presented as a reflection to Dominique was unconditional love. Imagine, love with no strings attached! It's amazing, because the classic third chakra person is always looking for the bottom line, the truth, with no strings attached.

When Dominique found a pure love, she accepted it into her life in recognition that she really could be that powerful and yet be in a relationship where Reese was not interested in taking any of her power or uniqueness, just in sharing life's experiences with her. Would you call this a great relationship? I would.

6 and 2
lost in a parking lot

Dan is an amazing man, a sixth chakra master of many trades, jack of none. He has lived in several countries and accomplished much in various fields. He is an exceptional healer, spiritual teacher and an amazingly perceptive (as a 6 would be) man. Anyone who has worked for him has developed admiration and respect for him as a leader, even those he's disciplined or fired.

His wife, Marian (2), was raised in a military family, and is made of great moral and spiritual strength in her own right. She has overcome many life challenges, and together they have become a very spiritual and successful couple.

Dan, as many 6's, can suffer from abstractions or what some people would misinterpret as daydreaming. The sixth chakra is another octave above the fifth, and as such any mentalisms that a 5 might suffer from are an order of magnitude higher for the 6 personality. Translation: Dan can get lost in a parking lot. No kidding. This is neither good nor bad, but Dan can have his mind in many places at once, not always all in this dimension.

I remember I was once in the car as a passenger when he was driving on a highway with two lanes in each direction. We were in the slow lane and there was a semi truck ahead of us in the same lane. On the back of the truck was a huge tailgate ramp, the kind that can be lowered to roll cargo on and off. Dan was blissfully unaware of the truck's presence. I carefully watched this scene unfold, knowing that Dan's abstractions of his sixth chakra were fully functioning and he was not grounded.

I waited until the last possible moment and, looking over my shoulder to check the other lane, grabbed the wheel from Dan to swerve to the left around the back of the truck that we had overtaken. Had I not done so, we would be wearing that huge tailgate ramp. He looked up, surprised, and I smiled at him. I wanted to see how deeply he was in that state of abstraction and he certainly was fully there!

When Dan realized what had just occurred, it surprised him. Had I not known his dominant chakra and his tendencies, the outcome of our drive would have been totally different.

How does his partner, Marian, reflect balance, presence, and being grounded back to Dan? The second chakra, as you recall, is the visceral chakra; the one most connected to the five senses. Her presence in his life helps him to root to this dimension, give him a feeling of security and a feeling of home, if you will; a place of repose for his very active mind.

To ground the 6 is to be more in the emotions. That is, as 5's must ground their physical bodies, 6's must go more into their hearts. It must be noted that I do not mean they should be more loving. Most 6's are by definition extremely loving. Grounding 6's is to make them more aware of their heart presence. Marian's presence, with her strong and emotionally stable second chakra, helps provide that grounding for Dan. She also helps him to see the big picture, even if it's only finding his way out of the parking lot.

How does Dan's 6 reflect back to Marian's 2? The sixth chakra is the inceptor of the new paradigm, a truth that no one has ever seen before. The 6 is the bringer of the new way of being and thinking, and the 2 is the shower of the higher vision.

Dan reflects what is highest and most noble about Marian, and his presence helps to remind her which goals in life take precedence over other goals. The 6 reflects to the 2 the highest possible image of herself that can be conceived or understood. Dan reflects to Marian the value of self-preciousness and self-validation, two qualities that the second chakra person comes to learn in a lifetime.

It has been said that a person's reach should always extend beyond their grasp. The 6 represents the unobtainable that is obtainable, but in new ways that challenge us to leave the paradigms that no longer serve us. The truth transcends all religious and dogmatic attempts to frame it.

Imagine living Dan's life. Would you want to be in the very small percentage of the population that is sixth chakra dominant?

3 and Various
a dating manipulator

I have counseled Janice (3) for many years though I've never met her. We've held our sessions by phone.

This is a story about manipulation. Before you make assumptions, realize that all third chakra dominant people are manipulators by definition (and that we all manipulate each other). Most of the time it is harmless and innocuous. The 3 has to learn what kind of manipulator to be.

It's about personal power and how to use it: 3's have a lifetime of learning how to use their personal power, not whether they have it. Some third chakra dominant people spend that lifetime hiding from their own power. Having a dominant third chakra is neither good nor bad; what you do with it is what defines the nature of your character, the same as any other chakra dominance.

In a phone session, I suddenly told Janice that I felt she dated men years younger than she is. She was startled, and admitted that it was true. I told her the reason why she did that was so that she could manipulate the men to avoid being in a position of vulnerability herself. By controlling the dating/relationship, Janice also avoided any real growth in herself because she never had a condition where she had to face the truth within herself.

In other words, she was living a lie. Not a severe one, but Janice was maintaining romantic relationships that precluded any emotional pain, or more directly, the pain of having to make an emotional decision, which is one of the key lessons the 3 comes to learn.

The men, probably of different chakra dispositions, would invariably reflect back to her a number of qualities. But in a higher sense, why do we date? If you've dated, you can probably come up with a few answers, but the more noble ones are about finding love, romance, a partnership, enjoying the company of someone, etc.

Do you suppose that eventually, in some way, Janice will learn her lesson about manipulation? That perhaps the lesson would come back to her in some reflection?

What if Janice met a man as powerful as she is, and she became dearly interested in him, regardless of age, and he was now the manipulator? What if she brings a man into her life who is as powerful as she is, they are both now interested in each other, but he is also alert to any manipulation she may attempt? This is another way of saying that we always bring the balance into our lives, in one way or another. It is inevitable to do so.

Buddha said that some of us take the steep, arduous, yet quick path up the mountain, while others take the gentle, sloping, yet longer path. The point is that we all make it to the top of the mountain.

Janice can live in her procrastination away from the truth of her own vulnerability to grow, but will pay a price for it. Any time we hold to an illusion, we suffer in any one or combination of those four archetypes of what it is to be human: mental, physical, emotional, and spiritual.

The suffering will externalize, as long as there is illusion. As long as Janice refuses to live her truth or avoids her own moral and ethical code, she is guaranteed to suffer in some manner, and will continue to bring the people into her life who will reflect the balance she inwardly seeks.

5 and Various
toxic and unavailable lovers

This case is somewhat complex and convoluted because there are several factors that create nuances. Here are some of the key points about Felicity (5-2), a beautiful, young and vibrant woman.

Felicity is single, and because of her stunning looks, can pretty much have her pick of men. And so, many men apply for the dating possibilities: from young to old, from single to married.

Why then, does she continue to date men who are married? Powerful, well-to-do men who are already in a relationship? Why does she date men who are unavailable for commitment? We've had several sessions, and in some Felicity says that she'll stop seeing this one particular man, but never seems to fully leave him.

The first answer may be the most obvious; date a married man and that way you are safe because he'll never leave his wife and so you won't have to get too emotionally attached. But is there something more?

What if you are a 5-2 and have some measure of abandonment issues mixed in with a level of constant ungroundedness. Wouldn't you require some form of constant reassurance, some strokes to assuage your feelings of fifth chakra lack of grounding and loneliness, and second chakra abandonment and the need for approval?

Mix in a bright mind that has lots of capability to worry endlessly about such things and you have Felicity's life. Does it sound like there's no hope for her? No, these are some of the ways the consciousness of a person externalizes the imbalances they perceive. Illusions, yes, but very powerful ones.

Do you think that Felicity can attract the reflective personalities into her life to help her heal? Do you suppose her sessions with me are part of that reflectivity?

If everything is fine, why does she again come for counseling about her relationships? Her job, family, and social life are OK, but could be better. Her family seems stable and she lives on her own. She has no real peers her age of the same sex. She works long, dedicated hours in her job and her social outlet is dating.

It would do Felicity well, I've told her, to strike up friendships with females her age with whom she can relax and be herself, with no need for approval or recognition - true friends.

Do you suppose if she does attract men into her life who represent her balance, that the married, unavailable man is one of them? Yes, he is. Whatever his chakra dominance, he is showing her the disconnect between her physical looks and her heart, between her idea of approval and the true approval that can only come from within. It's true some lessons are more stringent and painful than others, but they are lessons nonetheless.

Felicity will continue to draw reflections to her in this manner as long as the illusion exists. As she empowers herself by being more grounded, making better choices and loving herself fiercely, the relationships she encounters will change accordingly.

Do you suppose such people are scarred for life? No, there is no affect from which a person cannot heal. The higher Self is perfect, and if we don't get it in this lifetime, perhaps we will in the next.

Buddha said: "We are very much like the flame on a candle. The candle burns down and our flame is transferred to another candle. That candle burns down and our flame is transferred again. And again, and again."

We are the endless flame, and the candle is the body of the personality we experience in a given lifetime. When this body is complete and done, we will transfer our flame to another body, until there is no need to have a body.

4 and 4
left her husband for a woman

What can a heart chakra (4) dominant person give to another heart chakra person? If you will recall the section on same-chakra relationships, the pendulum can swing widely between happiness and suffering, but it always passes through the middle on the way to its zenith. That means there is always the opportunity for peace and balance in all relationships.

Carla, a 4 woman who had been married to Eduardo (5) for many years, suffered on and off from mild depression, and a lack of emotional communication with her partner. How does a person know when a relationship has reached the point where they must end it and move on? Such difficult questions reside in any of us who have had relationships where there were problems serious enough to contemplate such a drastic change.

As Carla had been experiencing the ups and downs of her own empathy, capability to give and to receive great love, and the lack of real emotional closeness that she was looking for, the whip-saw turbulence of her heart had driven her to make a decision to leave the relationship.

Could Eduardo, as fifth dominant, have done anything to prevent it? Again, such difficult questions are equally difficult to answer because of the constitution of each person, the desire to make things work, and the length of the marriage.

As far as I could perceive in counseling, Carla had most definitely reached the end point. But leaving Eduardo was one of the most difficult things she could have done. As a 4, when she is emotionally stressed, the first thing to go is the identity, the sense of Self. In her search for that place of inner peace and to calm the waves of depression that surged through her heart, she befriended another woman of her acquaintance, Lydia (4).

Eventually, what started out as a friendship of solace and understanding took a romantic turn, and Carla and Lydia discovered they had deep feelings for each other. They spent much time being honest with their feelings, Carla being careful not to fool herself that she might be on the rebound, but also desperately seeking a deeply-fulfilling relationship.

The boundaries that many societies place on same-sex relationships has not stopped them from taking place throughout history. Speaking metaphysically, love is love, and different spiritual teachers have varying viewpoints on same-sex relationships. I have never seen this to be a problem, standing in the way of one's evolution. The relationships we create are our own responsibility. As I often point out, the gurus say: "In the end it is between you and God," not you and your partner, society, family, etc.

As time went by, Carla and Lydia fell deeply in love and moved in together in a committed relationship. As of this writing, they are still happily together.

What could Lydia (4) offer Carla (4), that Eduardo (5) could not? Some answers are very easy. Eduardo could have been a very closed individual (perhaps ungrounded and emotionally distant), reflecting such closed-ness back to Carla that his fifth chakra stimulated her consciousness to a higher understanding (comprehension) of what she really desired in terms of a profoundly loving relationship. It stimulated her healthy emotional boundaries (though through years of tears, suffering, and self-denial) and helped her to forge an even stronger personal identity.

Though, as Carla left the relationship with Eduardo, she felt she had no idea of her personal identity, and her will to give love was at an extreme low. She spent much time in personal reflection and mild depression. Perhaps what she did know was that to preserve herself, she had to leave the relationship.

So, what did new love Lydia reflect back to Carla? The reinforcement of unconditional love, the deep empathy that Carla sought in her life, unfulfilled until now. The same chakra relationship can reinforce, like a sympathetic resonance, a desired quality if both people are willing to grow and do the spiritual work necessary to achieve that deep level of mutual love, affection, and partnership.

Although Carla still struggles with healthy emotional boundaries, those are also part of her life issues, which she would face no matter the relationship she created and reflected for herself.

As I often say, we all inevitably create relationships that reflect back to us the precise elements of the lessons we need to learn, so that we can overcome the illusion of separation.

4 and Earth
the shaman

I did a flower reading for a woman I'll call Shireen (4), and told her that in a past life she was an indigenous native man, a shaman in what is now Panama, 200 years before the building of the Panama Canal.

In that lifetime as a male shaman, she was living in concert with the earth, in harmony with the earth's resources, plants, and animals. It was a very good life and her position of shaman gave her much knowledge about the healing powers and properties of plants and herbs, and the totem representations of the animal kingdom as teachers of life and the interrelatedness of all things.

Shireen had known about the cycles of days and seasons and the rhythms and pulse of the earth and the life earth supports. She was living in concert with all that represented in a solemn, loving custodianship and acknowledgment of her place in the cosmos. Such an evolved life.

She later told me that in this life, the day her parents brought home their very first black and white TV, the first thing she saw was a documentary of the building of the Panama Canal. She said tears streamed down her face; a little girl watching TV for the first time seeing her former homeland being blown apart to make a huge ditch. She could not understand why such a thing would make her cry so.

In this lifetime, Shireen is a fourth chakra dominant woman. After lifetimes well-lived, a person can incarnate as a 4 with a great amount of purity of heart. Some 4's can also externalize a quality of the fourth chakra called the preserver or conserver. That is, they actively seek to preserve or conserve that which has purity, whether in other persons, buildings of antiquity, or of the earth and her resources.

Shireen is profoundly aware of the earth with respect to ecology and preservation. She has become a spiritual healer, continuing the tradition of her past life as a shaman. The earth reflects back to her a whole system of being, and as you know, the fourth chakra affects whole systems of the body (e.g., vascular, muscular, lymphatic, etc.). It is natural for Shireen to take a loving psychic relationship to what the earth represents as a holistic system, based on purity of function, and then for her to take another custodial relationship to the earth in this lifetime as she did in the past.

Left to itself, with no human beings, would the earth suffer pollution and global warming? Perhaps, if from some natural calamity as a volcano issuing millions of tons of ash into the atmosphere. But I think most would agree that our planet would be very, very pure; the absolute reflection of the aspirations of the heart chakra dominant person accepting the fact that they are that pure and that they really do represent the quality of what love is.

Did you know that the earth itself recognizes its role with humans in interesting ways? That the earth helps reflect back to us the balance we are looking for in our environment?

Consider these facts. In the Southwestern United States, people have many problems with dry skin because of the arid desert conditions of low humidity. There, aloe plants grow in abundance, the juice of which softens and moisturizes the skin.

In the Pacific Northwest where there is much dampness, there are pines and fir trees, the essential oils of which act as antiseptics for colds and to relieve congestion. The earth reflects back to us the balance we seek, within any chosen geography.

The earth has a consciousness, just as we do. We are her custodians and we are charged with the great responsibility of keeping the earth sacred and pure. If you look around you, it doesn't seem that we're doing a very good job.

But people like Shireen remind us of our responsibilities to keep purity intact, and the value in doing so. She reflects back to us the serious custodianship of earth that is all of our responsibility. Shireen emanates that quality of purity that evokes in us the desire to aspire to a greater part of our being-ness.

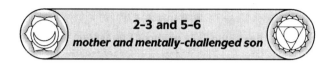

2-3 and 5-6
mother and mentally-challenged son

Michelle (2-3) is the mother of Gil (5-6), a mentally-challenged young man of about seventeen years of age. Michelle is a loving mother of two.

Gil consistently goes so far out of body that he requires constant care and supervision. I have counseled Michelle to work to get Gil back into his body as much as possible, to teach him regulated breathing techniques to slow down his racing and frenetic mind. It is difficult enough to teach the average 5 these techniques, but when you are the parent of a 5 adolescent who is also challenged, the responsibilities and requirements are extreme.

I have done spiritual healing work on Gil, and many of his issues stem from the way the consciousness flows through his fifth chakra in this lifetime. For some like Gil, the emanation of the quality of his being never fully touches down on the earth plane, so the result is a person who is not always "totally there."

Doing healing work of such a nature is never a sure thing, which is a very difficult thing to convey to concerned parents. I have visited children's hospitals to work on terminally ill children, and then have told the parents that I've done the best I can, but the child's higher Self and God have an arrangement that I cannot alter. I can only help facilitate the connection between the children and their own higher Self (God connection). In many cases I have been successful; in some I have not.

In spiritual healing, you cannot show a slide, x-ray, or cell culture to someone or surgically remove the problem organ or tissue. In spiritual healing, one must take into account what I call the "whole human being." While it is entirely possible to heal any disease or infirmity, it is not always the case.

There are three main reasons why people do not instantly heal: mission statement, karma, and free will. It may be the person's mission statement to have an infirmity for a certain length of time, and no healer, no matter how good, can affect a change if none is within the mission statement of that person.

If there is a karmic reason for the illness, sometimes people will go through a litany of healers; not to heal the disease but for the development of their character in the stamina it takes to look for the cure itself. Remember, effort, not goals, is what defines the character of an individual.

And, there's free will. It is possible that a person can will themselves not to heal for a variety of reasons. Not very common, but possible.

As I worked on Gil's fifth and sixth chakras, I noticed several small interruptions in the flow of consciousness through the lens of the chakra and through the shushumna. I have met with some limited success, but I suspect this is a life issue for Gil, and therefore for his mother.

What lessons is Gil reflecting back to Michelle? What does a 5-6 have to reflect back to a 2-3? The 5 articulates what humanity cannot yet know and the 6 incepts the paradigms that no one has yet seen on the earth plane. Perhaps at the least Gil is cultivating patience and focus as a reflection to Michelle. 2's can be very chaotic and unfocused, and with a 2-3 reference they can be unfocused and insist they are right about it, if in the lower aspects.

The 5 increases the level of understanding in others. Perhaps as Michelle is a full-time mother and custodian for Gil, she is learning compassion and yielding other priorities in life for the priority of her family and its well-being.

Perhaps Michelle is learning the focus through faith, that somehow Gil is reflecting back her own inner trust that the healthcare bills and the regular bills of the household will be met.

Michelle is married, and her husband Ron (3) is a kind, loving and attentive man to Gil. Perhaps also, Ron provides the reflection of that rational and pragmatic emanation of his third chakra to her, so that she does not become emotionally overwhelmed - a lower aspect of the second chakra when faced with too many multiple shared priorities and responsibilities, especially if they are obligations to other people.

What does Michelle reflect back to her son? Support, as only a 2 can. The second chakra is creativity, but it is also burdens and responsibility. Many are the second chakra people who justified their existence and sacrificed their integrity by taking on too many promises to other people's goals at the expense of their own, and by that same loyalty to others over themselves fell apart from too much responsibility and too many burdens.

Ironically, those same overwhelmed 2's would reason they simply were not working hard enough, so they worked even harder. This was not the answer to their problem, but many second chakra people do it all the time because they have not yet placed enough value on themselves, as whole and complete, and looked to their completion by serving others.

Michelle reflects to Gil infinite possibilities. What dashes the hopes of a parent more than an ill child? Don't parents wish to see their children outlive, outdo, etc., what they have done? The second chakra is ever evolving and represents infinite creativity, but remember, your chakras are "on" at all times because they are inter-dimensional and not limited by space and time - you on a higher level.

The quality of Michelle's second chakra, especially if she is living her life well, is emanating to Gil the limitless possibilities of life: that there are many ways to accomplish a goal.

Even though it may appear that Gil is only making minor progress, there is a higher part of him that is receiving fully all the love and attention that Michelle offers. I've mentioned there is no stronger karma than that of parent/child. The more Michelle trusts in herself, the more dharma is created for the entire family karma to relieve itself.

It may be this way for the rest of Gil's life, but look at the wonderful parents he reflected back to himself. Is he a teacher to Michelle, or is Michelle the teacher? They both are to each other, reflecting precisely the properties of consciousness to restore balance from the illusion of separation.

3 and 2
she does everything "right"
and it still doesn't work

Amy is a 3 and a very successful professional. She's married to Drake (2) who is also a successful professional. Together they've had many years of marriage, children, and adventures.

Yet Amy divorced Drake, after much inner conflict. She had procrastinated for years from making the emotional decision, as many 3's do. But as a bright and articulate person, how could she have waited so long before making the decision to end the marriage?

Drake, while very successful and compassionate, is pretty stuck in his ways. As a 2, he's become very controlling in emotional affairs of the heart, assuming his very high intellect and profession are his first priorities. Effectively what he did was insulate himself away from Amy's affections.

They have attempted reconciliation. They've each had spiritual counseling sessions with me. But after Amy initiated the divorce proceedings, Drake became vindictive, showing many examples of what the lower aspect of the second chakra can be.

It took much courage for Amy to finally make the move. She even moved away from town and took one of her adult children with her. By now, she is more stable and making a life of her own, slowly but surely. But how could she have been so deeply affected by the divorce, which she initiated? Did she not see it coming?

Things like this do not happen overnight. By the time there's a divorce, something has been brewing below the surface a long time before it became a real issue. Many of us do not listen to our hearts for the subtle cues that something is not quite right. We deny or make excuses, or assume everything will work out all right if we just make peace.

In Amy's case as a 3, she procrastinated making the emotional decisions that her inner truth revealed to her years ago. But similar to a 2, she also is an extremely loyal and traditional woman, seeking to save her marriage to a man (whom I feel she still deeply loves in spite of everything) who has become the most analytical of 2's.

Drake had taken his professional passion and sharpened it to a fine edge. Part of that is easy, because most professions do not require emotional intimacy. But in his intimate life, he took that analytical capability and used it as a tool to insulate himself from exposing the soft vulnerability of his true Self. A sentimental romantic lies somewhere below all that rigid inflexibility and Amy knew it. She knew it when she married him. That's part of the reason *why* she married him.

Things sometime change ever so slowly over time. So slowly, like the growth of a tree, that we don't notice until the tree is shading the house. This is why emotional communication is so very important. Don't assume your partner knows how you feel, and don't allow (in some loving way) your partner to refuse you emotional communication.

What is Drake reflecting back to Amy in his lower aspect of 2? How does vindictiveness help a relationship? You cannot control the actions of others, but you do have a free-will choice as to how you will react to them. Drake reacted to the divorce as a power-struggle, an act to wrest who's in control as the lower aspect of the second chakra can be very controlling.

Reflected to Amy, this would help (over time) to firm her resolve to make an emotional decision by Drake's rigidity and inflexibility (lower aspect of second chakra "no choice"). In a way Drake's reticence to show emotional love helped Amy to see that there are alternatives to living in the manner she did, even though it was painful to change it. In another way he showed Amy that she really does have choices, many of them.

Amy would show Drake, first of all, that people cannot truly be controlled or treated as fellow professionals when in an intimate environment such as a marriage. The third chakra of Amy reflects back to Drake's second what personal power is, and the individuation of choice.

How long do you think Drake will dwell in his vindictiveness? Do you think he may be in denial, justifying and reinforcing his actions while not addressing the key issues that led to this place of suffering?

Do you think that Amy actually did a service to Drake by divorcing him? It may be that Drake will not comprehend, as brilliant as he is, that lesson for a very long time. Again, sometimes the brilliant mind is a real impediment to true spiritual growth.

Amy did everything she could to save the marriage. She was resourceful in the way the third chakra can be, even though eventually it was to no avail for the marriage itself. But the experience of making the effort did teach Amy there indeed *are* alternatives; that there is always a choice.

It also taught her the value of her own opinion, which in a tongue-in-cheek manner the third chakra person is incarnated to give others, based on the uniqueness of their grasp of the truth.

2 and 3
mother/doctor and son's
disappearing tumor

Katherine is a 2, a doctor and mother to Alan (3), her adult son. Alan was diagnosed with a tumor on his liver. She brought him to me for spiritual healing the evening before his hospital appointment to have the tumor biopsied to determine if there was a malignancy.

Alan is very much a 3; a self-assured truth giver, immersed in the technology industry, a little skeptical of spiritual things like the work that I do, and dealing with much suppressed anger. I told him where the tumor was on his liver and what brought it about.

Often, a third chakra individual will gather anger like a room gathers dust. Most often it is impersonal, but a 3 can take things *very* personally. The anger usually resides in the solid and hollow organs in the mid-section of the body, the gastro-intestinal tract, and can affect (among other things) the biochemistry of the body and the thyroid. I have made these observations through many spiritual counseling sessions over the years.

In this case, Alan's tumor was the result of unexpressed anger at any iniquities or injustices he experienced in his life; especially those related to his emotions. I told him the tumor originated some years ago and gave him the reasons why. After counseling him on how to make sure the tumor did not return, I did spiritual healing on him.

A week later I heard from Katherine. She said the doctors had performed the biopsy on Alan the morning after I saw him. She also said the reason it took a week for the doctors to get back to her was because of their confusion. They told her that when they performed the surgery to remove a portion of the tumor, there was no tumor to be found. It had completely disappeared.

Of course Katherine was relieved to hear that Alan was able to completely release the tumor, and that our healing session had some good effect. It is very important to note that any disease or infirmity can come back; the possibility for its appearance is always there.

In Alan's case, his tumor did come back some two years later. I asked Katherine if Alan had been applying what I instructed him to do. She answered "No." So he was able to create the same conditions, through unresolved anger, that allowed another tumor to come into existence on his liver.

And so, sometimes we do not learn our lessons, even when we overcome a challenge as dramatically as Alan did. He still did not manage his anger, he continued to procrastinate against emotional decisions, and he could not let go of his feelings around certain issues. So the infirmity reappeared in his life.

What did Katherine reflect to Alan? She was already a healthcare provider – a doctor. She was already offering him the best possible care as a mother and a professional. Why bring him to me?

Katherine's second chakra represents infinite alternatives, the power of the ever-renewing aspect of our existence that allows for the possibility of something new and unexpected to appear, when all possibilities seem to be exhausted. The 2 is the one who brings something forth from nothing.

The 2 offers alternatives where there are none. The skeptic that is Alan allowed Katherine to offer him alternatives he may not have even considered because of the possibility of something serious that could develop from a tumor. Spiritual healing is difficult to understand, because it is not bound by temporal and spatial laws of physics and biochemistry.

The fact that Katherine, as a doctor, offered healing alternatives, at the least offered to Alan the possibility that he could be healed in ways the skeptic (searcher for truth) in him could not yet understand.

2's often have a bigger picture of what is "real" and possible, and sometimes they suffer terribly for it because no one believes their vision. Sometimes they stifle their own great inspirations because they doubt that such a powerful (and accurate) vision of what could be simply could not be possible or obtainable. Hence, the valuable lesson of faith that they learn for themselves is exactly the same lesson they teach to the world.

If people come to me in one of my many healing workshops and ask if I teach "faith" healing, I tell them "Yes! It takes great faith, an absolute confidence and fidelity of knowingness that the higher nature of Self exists, to be a good spiritual healer, and to make that higher level of consciousness exist in this dimension. You cannot fake it."

Katherine's second chakra faith brought her to me, and hence her son to me. His psychic relationship to her meant that he is to learn a measure of faith in this lifetime, and that this particular chapter in his life is one opportunity to do so. The opportunity has come up again, and may do so several times before he "gets it."

What is Alan reflecting back to Katherine? We know that he is a 3, a manipulator and manifestor by definition. But a 2 is a controller and a creator by definition.

What is the difference between manifesting (3) and creating (2)? Creating is to bring something forth from where nothing exists; to offer infinite alternatives. Manifestation is alchemically combining the mental, physical, emotional, and spiritual aspects of what it is to be a human being into any combination. Manifestation is manipulation of energy: it is transformation and translation, like the currency exchange transforming one country's money into another country's currency.

This is part of the reason why 3's are such great manipulators, but also why they can manifest material things, like money.

Alan reflects personal power back to Katherine. Where she might spread herself too thin among various healing alternatives and may offer many alternatives to Alan, he also represents the truth of personal power to Katherine.

That means that any healing alternative that had no truth would fall away from Alan's awareness, discarded as a less-than-true alternative.

Alan's 3 offers to Katherine the kernel of individuation of choice. As Alan is a powerful skeptic, living in the world of technological science, he engenders in part the rigors of scientific thought that helps Katherine to be more emotionally grounded and therefore more powerful in her choices for herself and for her son.

That would help her avoid being emotionally overwhelmed by the very choices she seeks to offer, and helps to prevent her from going into the role of "rescuer" as so many 2's can do. They intuitively have the psychic answer for so many people around them, so it's easy to fall in to that rescuer trap.

On some higher level of his being, Alan knows exactly what he is doing and why he created the lessons he has. But it may take him many cycles to overcome the internalization of anger against the iniquities of the world and taking things too personally.

Perhaps part of Katherine's second chakra lesson being reflected back from Alan is that of true compassion: allowing someone to suffer, if they must, in order to learn their lesson. Even if that lesson is a life lesson, there is a part of Katherine that has to learn when not to be Alan's rescuer, or anyone else's.

5 and 2
*marries the man who killed her
in a past life*

This story may challenge your belief system. I was holding a past life, karma, and reincarnation workshop for a group of twelve. After the lecture I conducted past life evaluations for all attendees.

During the evaluation for one woman, let's call her Diana, I said that she was married to a man in a past life who strangled and killed her.

The evaluation got very interesting when I told her that in this lifetime she found the same man and married him again!

Could you imagine being Diana, hearing this? And perhaps having an answer why she doesn't like anything tight around her neck in this lifetime?

Diana, who is a 5, told me that the man she married in this lifetime, Evan (2), had already tried to kill her by strangling her. She told me this happened some years ago but that she is still married to him.

What quality within her would make her stay? Why would she invite the same karma into her life in the person of the same man who killed her in a past life relationship? How do you think she felt when she put all the pieces together?

Diana incarnated again to have the same relationship with the man who killed her. Only in this lifetime he did not go through with it.

As a 5, what was she reflecting back to Evan in this lifetime? What qualities of the fifth chakra help a person to learn to reign in their passion and rage? The 5 represents comprehension and understanding, but ever more so effective if they are very grounded.

Imagine the personal fortitude Diana would have to have, when leaving her body in the last lifetime of being strangled, not to attach in the astral plane to the violence and rage she felt from Evan.

Imagine the strength of Diana's soul-purpose in this lifetime to find Evan once again, and to take the chance that the murder could happen again.

The grounded and evolved Diana reflected a higher level of awareness to Evan. She was able in her awareness, mentally, emotionally, and psychically, to mollify his rage through the 95% of communication that is the emanation of one's consciousness.

She "saw" how he could be as whole and complete, as perfect; as his second chakra normally would for others, but she saw it as a compassionate comprehension of the true Evan beyond rage. She gave his rage a place to blow through without being affected by it. Such inner strength.

And what, in Evan's karma, would allow him to have committed a murder in one lifetime, yet reincarnate to find the same woman to see if he would make the same intense karma again? Can you imagine the karma from killing another person? It must be reconciled - either in this lifetime or another.

What did Evan reflect back to Diana? As a 2 he reflected the opportunity for her to express her compassion in the form of healing the relationship. Do you think that Diana really needed to reincarnate, being the one who was murdered? Or would it be Evan who must reincarnate to pay his spiritual, karmic debt?

The second chakra reflects the creative aspect of the universe, but we do not fully understand it. Remember, an epiphany that can be understood ahead of time is not an epiphany. It must be that *qualitative* step of faith into a future that your heart can feel, but your physical mind cannot know. That is where true spiritual growth is.

Evan, even as reincarnated with the karmic guilt of murder, still represented as a reflection to Diana that her faith could be strong enough to see him truly, that he will not be the one given to rage through passion in this lifetime, that he will overcome his rage, guilt, and karma.

And what about Diana being fifth chakra dominant in this lifetime with Evan going right for where her dominant chakra is located again (at the throat)?

Is that like trying to stifle the very thing that can reflect back to you your own healing in the consciousness of another person?

The fifth chakra is located in the throat area because it represents higher forms of communication, teaching, comprehension, and understanding. How ironic is it that Diana would be attacked in the same place that is her dominant feature of her consciousness in this lifetime.

Would his act of choking her be a symbol of him playing out and trying to stifle the greatest fear of the throat chakra lesson he is reflecting back to himself (No one knows me for who I truly am. No one can see the root of my rage.)?

Can you see how this is like a moebius strip (a loop of paper with a half twist in it) of logic that constantly comes back on itself, endlessly to repeat until the lesson is fully learned, the illusion is overcome?

In their mutual dance of consciousness Diana and Evan overcame a tremendous obstacle of violence and guilt through forgiveness, compassion, and clear vision. How many of us would have the courage to reincarnate with such a mission?

Think of this universe as a collaborative universe. You do, in part, pick where, when, and with whom you'll incarnate, along with many other criteria, in collaboration with God, that seamlessly connected part of your higher Self. Imagine the elegance that exists within you, ready at any time to be realized and brought forth into expression.

Know also, that when you reincarnate, two things happen: 1) You always incarnate having the ability and the strength to desolve past life karma. 2) You do not reincarnate alone. Other people incarnate to help you deal with your karma. You meet them at key points in your life through your dominant chakra attactions.

2 and 4
ancient wisdom living in balance

In the Pacific Northwest there are many carved wooden artifacts from the indigenous people that depict a man being devoured by a bear, or being eaten by an orca (killer whale). Most uninitiated archeologists and anthropologists, trained in the secular world, assumed a rather bloody end had come to some of these poor fellows. They postulated that perhaps these were some of the dangers the nation's first cultures experienced in their tribal lives.

The real story is quite different. The shamans knew that the only way they could understand the bear was to become one. They knew that the only way to understand orcas was to become an orca. They metaphorically had to die so they could be reborn.

Put another way, they had to allow their ego to be fully consumed, to allow their spirit nature to guide them, before they could know the essence of the bear or the orca. To know the wisdom of the animal, they had to become the animal. These are deeply spiritual teachings and metaphysical understandings of the balance of nature that have been marginalized today by our modern materialism and empiricism.

The first people assumed and knew their position well in the balance, the web, of life. They knew that all nature has a system by which balance could be found, restored, maintained.

Many of those people understood that whenever they had a problem, the best thing to do was to start over from a point of balance they knew to be sure. Perhaps it involved going into the mountains on a three or four-day fast, to sit in nature, absorb its balance and to meditate upon that balance. Parents knew what to do when their children were full of too much energy; they would sit them on a big rock to draw them down more into the earth.

Those lifetimes are in you and me. We've lived them. *We are them.*

Picture Crystal, a second chakra dominant woman, who has had several lifetimes as an indigenous person, often living in forested areas abounding with water. Food was plentiful, war was uncommon but skirmishes possible here and there; balance was essential to the harmony of the tribe's welfare.

In this lifetime, Crystal has a daughter, Rihanna (4) about seven years old, whose heart is very pure. One thing to recognize about 4's is, it's not that they do not feel deeply enough, it's that they feel only all too well.

Rihanna also had past lifetimes in the same eras as her mother, sometimes changing roles with her. In a past life Rihanna was Crystal's mother.

Crystal has seen me for spiritual counseling and had many questions about how best to raise her daughter in the modern day environment. How best can Crystal parent Rihanna in this lifetime, given the past life information and current chakra dispositions?

Rihanna gets it. She understands much already, but she retains the purity of her heart, already a deep love of earth and her resources, and the recapitulation of her past lives lived very near where she lives now, in the Pacific Northwest. Crystal's second chakra can hold a safe place for Rihanna, in that the 2 recognizes the need for sacredness, ceremony and ritual to honor that which is holy within one's Self. Perhaps not all 2's know this consciously, but those seeds are in everyone who has a second chakra, which means *all of us.*

Crystal's second chakra reminds (reflects to) Rihanna of her sacredness, but also of her self-worth and hence, healthy emotional boundaries. These are two feminine-chakra dominant people. If you will recall from the section on even-even chakras, they are very emotionally-based chakras. The 2 seeks through desire of their passions: the 4 seeks through the quality of love. The 2 shows the 4 the vibrant colors and weave of the many threads in the tapestry of life; what there is that's worth living for.

Crystal's second chakra is awakening in Rihanna a stronger sense of the passion for life, which also helps Rihanna to exhibit healthy emotional boundaries. Crystal has expressed to me her desire to help keep Rihanna's environment as pure as possible (that means little TV, lots of natural, healthy foods, and a healthy atmosphere or home-life for her to grow).

Rihanna is responding by showing a very balanced demeanor, but it is also due to her past lives lived in much harmony with her environment. Remember that many 4's are interested in some form of ecology, preservation or conservation, whether it is in the physical environment of the world, or with people, animals, etc. It will externalize in some fashion.

Like our story of the two schoolteachers (each a 5) who had a loving life as sisters in Lucern, Switzerland in the past, and reunited, Crystal and Rihanna also came back together in this lifetime to experience each other again.

Crystal will continue to nurture a safe and loving environment that will always echo the balance of nature from the past. The tradition of sacredness will continue.

4 and Family
breaking cultural karma

Jade is a 4, a very sweet and loving young woman with a very strong family cultural karma. She was in an arranged marriage to a man who lives in India. The family arrangement was for her to go there, marry him, live with him for a year, then come back to this country and bring him over under the benefit of her existing U.S. citizenship and their married status.

Jade is a deeply spiritual woman who prays diligently every day and has always been a very well-loved family-oriented person. She is a 4 in the sense of the inner purity and harmlessness that radiates from her. It doesn't take a spiritually attuned person to see these qualities in her.

When she returned from her year in India, having married and spent time with the man, her heart wrestled with indecision because she knew she did not love him. How could she have taken part in an arranged marriage to a man whom she did not love? Out of devotion to her family and her culture, which regularly practiced this form of pairing couples? Jade's family is also deeply religious and believes these cultural customs are in keeping with their religion.

Initially, some members of Jade's family had arranged a private session with me to talk about various subjects, including their concern for Jade's happiness. They said that she had been in mild forms of depression since her marriage, but that she was doing her best to be happy, and maintained her prayers for some three hours a day. Yes, *three* hours a day. As best I could, I counseled them about her without the benefit of Jade being present.

Soon after, Jade herself made an appointment to see me. She lamented of her condition; feeling trapped and overwhelmed between family harmony, marriage to her new husband, maintaining the cultural karma, her ardent prayers.

How could she go against centuries of cultural karma, and not love the man whom she was arranged to marry? Why could she not just accept her situation as a blessing and maintain the family harmony? Because she truly did not love this man, and was slowly destroying herself from the inside out.

Jade's family deeply loves her, but her mother would say to her "You are killing your mother and father (us)" or "You are causing us to get sick and die early" and "We are praying for you that you are well and happy."

Sending such powerful guilt and mixed messages is a great burden for one (Jade) who is already empathic by her fourth chakra nature. Imagine the incredible emotional pressure and veiled emotional blackmail ("you're killing us") that she had to endure.

She would ask me if she was doing the right thing; she most seriously did not want to offend anyone and seemed to be in an impossible position where any decision she made would cause someone discomfort. And, fourth chakra persons can feel this way: nowhere to turn, no options without severe consequences.

I advised her that her decisions are best served when in fidelity to her Creator. Again: "In the end, it is between you and God." This seemed to have a limited effect, as she must learn to preserve her own purity as much as she wished to preserve that which is pure of her marriage, family, and culture. Without fidelity to her own feelings, her own moral and ethical code, how could she represent a good relationship to anyone?

It takes great courage for a single individual to break a cultural karma: centuries of attachment to a religious tenet that edicts the quality of your life's spirituality is tied to your conformity with the consensus of the religious culture.

What do you suspect Jade did? She later ran away from her family (with whom she was living) in the self-preservation sense. Just before that, she made a mild attempt at suicide as an act of desperation and frustration at what the fourth chakra comes to learn - emotional communication.

No matter what she did, she could not communicate to her family that she simply was not in love. Her family was honestly concerned for her physical and emotional well-being, but they absolutely could not see beyond the heavy veil of the karma that brought these events to pass. In their mind still, it is Jade who needs the help.

I had advised Jade to develop friendships with other women who did not want anything from her, just social friends. She did this, and found some relief from the incessant emotional pressure of her parents and siblings.

I also told her a quote from Paramhansa Yogananda: "When it comes down to a choice between family and God, you always pick God." That means that by serving God you really are serving your family in the best way possible, in fidelity to your own inner knower.

Jade's fourth chakra dominance was here in this incarnation as being the quality of what love is. Love is unconditional and does not know race or cultural differences. The Buddhists have a saying: "God picks you; you don't pick God." In cases of love, a man-made arrangement for Jade did not resonate with the strings of her heart. But love is blind.

Why did she not love this man? Do you suppose you could love someone you were told to love? Wouldn't you rather let love dance freely through the open blossoms of your heart; occurring when it will, to its own rhythm and measure, and not to a pre-arranged cultural, man-made agenda?

Even though the family is still caught up in the hysteria of her well-being, Jade has contacted me from time to time to say that she is well and living one day at a time. She has contacted her family, through friends, to let them know that she is OK and sorting things out. She will return to them when she is ready, and I applaud her character.

So it can be for fourth chakra people in such overwhelming circumstances. Everyone around her, with the exception of some of her friends, has applied such pressure that they thought was loving, but the bottom line was to bring her back into the family and culture that was her karma. They reflected to Jade love, family, harmony, and a good morality. But it just did not match with the desires of Jade's heart.

Being in a marriage to a man she did not love really triggered and reflected her powers of self-preservation, made her look at her inner purity and what it was worth to her, and made her examine how much value she placed on her own integrity (healthy emotional boundaries).

Many fourth chakra people make peace in order to achieve harmony in their relationships. They don't realize how much of their integrity they give away.

Do you think your inner qualities are balanced if you sacrifice your integrity for the sake of your family, your wife/husband/partner, your culture?

Not all examples are as extreme as Jade's situation. Most cultures no longer have arranged marriages. Imagine the internal fortitude that Jade mustered to bring this situation about, on some higher level of her being, so that she could exercise her free will to either capitulate and continue the cultural karma, or stand fast in her integrity and break centuries of tradition in order to preserve her own purity of heart. Which action, on Jade's part, do you think serves the greater good?

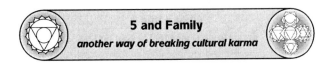

5 and Family
another way of breaking cultural karma

Adja (5) came to me for a spiritual counseling session to talk about her love for a special man. She is Punjabi (northwestern India region), and comes from a strong cultural karma similar to the previous case history. Adja told me that the man she loved is white, and what did I think about her considering marrying him?

I asked about her family, their traditions, and how she supposed they would react. She replied that they would be violently against such a union. The mixing of races was not something to be considered lightly, but here again we have a situation where a fifth chakra consciousness was here in this lifetime as teacher of understanding and compassion.

How brave Adja is, though she may have felt the love for her Caucasian partner was greater than herself, with no initial thought of how her family would react. And of course it is possible that some people marry deliberately to choose something their parents don't approve of, but not in these cases. Simply, Adja fell in love, and the man happened to be white.

In understanding spirituality and karma, the strongest forms of karma are parental (you and your parents, you and your children) and familial karma (the one you marry, and your biological and collective families).

For Adja to break a cultural karma, one in which her parents and family were steeped, was a great and singular act, for there was no support for her decision, which is why she came to see me.

In these cases I am always reminded of what Paramhansa Yogananda said: "When it comes down to a choice between God and family, you always pick God." That means, the only way you can really help your family is to choose God. Some people think of the religious connotations of what God represents, and you can view the many world's religions and see how God is viewed differently. But to each of us there is a higher principle, I like to call it God, which represents a perfected form existing in pure love, compassion, and harmlessness.

If Adja were to act in accordance with her heart (her higher intuition), that is her personal alignment to what God represents to her. Because she is strong in her 5th chakra (throat) the "to do" and "to learn" aspects are in play.

That is, she is learning one of the lessons that the throat chakra teaches, which is not whether she has intuition, but whether she is trusting it and not flurrying through the many thoughts, ramifications, and repercussions swirling through her head. Throat chakra tends to make one "think about what they're thinking about" or puts them in their head too much and hence out of body.

If you remember, the spirituality of our lives is all about *balance* and the effort we make to maintain it. If Adja spends too much time in thought or going out of body, it puts her in an out-of-balance position and creates problems. In order for her to be in balance, she is learning to trust what her intuition is already telling her.

Her "to do" is as a teacher. By taking this position with her Caucasian husband through honest love, Adja is offering the lesson to her parents and family by breaking the cultural karma held firmly in place by tradition for centuries. In some cultures, running off to marry someone or marrying out of race was (and still is) a very serious crime, and punishable.

Is it really teaching? Is it perceived by Adja's family that she is teaching them something about free will, conscious choice and the equanimity of love? Perhaps not, judging by their severe reaction to her announcement. They may not, in their lifetime, understand Adja's actions, but it illustrates the point of spirituality that at the same time makes it so difficult: we must each face our inner truth and rise above ego and karmic attachments.

Our chakras are us, and in them are the seeds of karma; guaranteeing that we will create conditions and circumstances in our lives that offer us the opportunity to overcome the ego and karma. One of my teachers would say that it's better to face your karma now than to put it off for later, or worse, to wait for the next lifetime.

The change that Adja made in her life was courageous; to face a seemingly unending stream of disapproval from her parents, family, and friends. Sometimes, when you make a spiritual choice, such is the outcome - you cannot make anyone understand you or your motivation, though you yourself may be clear. You can teach the lesson, but the students must also be ready to receive, and perhaps Adja's family was not yet in a place to understand her actions and motivations.

In the time since Adja came to me for counseling, she did marry the Caucasian man and they had a baby. She continues in her life, confident of choices made with an inner trust.

2 and 3
a classic 2-3 relationship

Emil (2) and Monica (3) are a great couple in their early 30's. They own two successful tattoo studios and have many good friends. I have had the opportunity to counsel them separately and together, and have also enjoyed their company as friends.

Monica's story is that she was at a party and sometime later in the evening, Emil had nodded off to sleep in her lap. She gazed down upon his face and was shocked with the feeling, "uh oh, I think I love this man." From that moment on, Monica knew she was hooked, and fell deeply in love with Emil.

Today, they have a beautiful daughter, and their businesses are thriving. Their outlook is optimistic, realistic, but they are eager to learn about their spiritual nature. Emil and Monica invited me to do flower readings at one of their businesses. It was so popular, we had to turn people away.

Typically, Emil as a (2) would be showing Monica the big picture and would have trouble manifesting it for himself, by himself. Monica, as a (3) would be helping Emil to individuate his power and to make value-related decisions based more on his personal power.

In their relationship, they do exactly that. Emil's 2nd chakra teaches the lesson of faith and of not being the single person responsible for everyone's happiness. Emil is such a giver that he exhausts himself emotionally doing so.

Being smart enough to say "yes" to the relationship meant he married a strong woman who is also 3rd chakra dominant: a combination that leads Monica into conflicts (non-violent) and power struggles in her business, and sometimes, social life.

Monica is the spiritual leader and sets the tone for their home life, business life, and even their social life. Because Emil has matured in his total love for Monica, he is not threatened by her lead.

This also means Emil can make fine decisions in all three categories, but Monica tends to set the spiritual tone or foundation for the rest to transpire.

An example is when the establishment of their second business was blocked by the small town council, which let it be known that a tattoo and piercing business in the center of the town wasn't in accord with their standards. Monica went head-to-head with the city elders, successfully made her case, and established the business, which is doing quite well.

The 3rd chakra has the tendency to induce the search for higher levels of truth in the individual to the extent it influences (as consciousness) the circumstances and settings to that end. Monica was bound to start a business in that small town and found a way: the 3rd chakra can manifest. Manifest does not mean to create (2nd chakra), it manipulates the energy to transform one thing into something else.

Emil is extremely talented as an artist; a real visionary. He not only has the innate artistic ability to draw on paper or skin in superb detail, he also intuits the true needs of the customer.

A tattoo is a highly personal and intimate endeavor. Most people have a very strong emotional connection in their motivation to be tattooed.

As a couple, Emil is highly intelligent and allows Monica ample room to manifest their successes, but he is also flexible and plays his part of the relationship as a 2nd chakra can, with great passion and lust for life.

Monica is spontaneous and gregarious, and I noted several of their friendships are very deep. She dearly loves Emil, and he allows her to love him deeply.

Together, these two have a very solid 2 and 3 relationship, and I see it will only deepen with time.

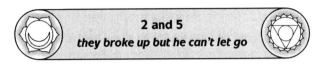

2 and 5
they broke up but he can't let go

Imagine a relationship that has all the characteristics of a deep and committed nature. Lots of tender love, two spiritually-aware people, and yet somehow the relationship still fails.

I had the opportunity to counsel Ralph (2) and Katrina (5) over the years. This couple even gifted each other to have spiritual counseling sessions with me.

Ralph had been studying metaphysics and the spiritual nature of the human being for a while. He met Katrina a couple of years prior and instantly fell for her. Katrina displays a lot of 4th chakra qualities of lovingness and empathy for others, even though she is really 5th chakra dominant. She too had been studying metaphysics and relationship dynamics in couples for a long time.

Katrina had experienced a divorce in her life before meeting Ralph, and that experience had caused her to examine how couples might go through a divorce process more smoothly and lovingly. So she wrote a book on the subject, as it affects both parties and any children who are involved. She had taken adversity in her life and turned it into a loving way to help couples that no longer desire to share their lives with each other. Such courage is commendable.

After dating for awhile, Ralph and Katrina became very close to the point where they were in love. They went out together, visited each other's homes, but were not yet living together.

Ralph was extremely conscientious and attentive to Katrina, to the extent he would anticipate Katrina's needs, frequently initiate communications, and gift her with small tokens of his love.

A little after a year, Ralph noted that there was a definite shift, and that Katrina did not seem to be responding to him as before. He felt she was being more guarded and less direct in her communications with him. He even sensed that their relationship was unraveling. This was not his desire, for he was deeply in love with Katrina.

Over a little more time, it became obvious that the relationship was over, but the understanding of why it was over escaped Ralph, so he came to me for guidance. I had not heard from Katrina during this period, so cannot say her reasons for the shift to terminate the relationship.

One of the most difficult things about relationships that end is the "why" question. The reason it is so difficult is that we can know for ourselves our own motivations for our actions, and we can even extrapolate to a certain degree our partner's actions, but that does not speak for them.

In intimate relationships, there are two free wills; two individuals composed of their own motivations, desires, and karma and chakra dominance. When relationships end and one asks "why" it partly reveals that the other partner has his/her own free will to decide in a manner that may not be fully understood. The "why" question may never be answered, as Katrina's distancing and lack of direct communication with Ralph left him in the dark.

Since Ralph has a strong 2nd chakra, he is likely to be the classical visionary, both wanting and desiring to see the big picture in life for himself, but also valuing his life in terms of how he sees the big picture for others - especially in intimate relationships.

Ralph could have over-analyzed, smothered and scrutinized Katrina to the point where she felt overwhelmed by his good intentions. There are many times where the 2nd chakra person (Ralph) can suffer because his own good intentions to help others does not take into consideration others' reaction to those intentions.

It very well could be that Katrina (5th chakra) felt a little too grounded by Ralph's attentions. Katrina has the characteristics of using her 5th and 4th chakra, so she can live in a very emotionally-charged state of being. As you may recall, when two feminine-based chakras (e.g., 2nd and 4th) are in relationship, it can be really good or really emotionally charged. Perhaps Katrina felt in a state of overwhelm from Ralph without Ralph fully realizing that his good intentions were not giving Katrina the space she felt she required in her life.

Imagine too, that Katrina's book is about how to best survive the divorce process, and you know a couple does not have to be married to experience the pain of separation when the relationship ends.

Should Katrina have been more grounded in the 5th chakra? Should Ralph in his 2nd chakra have restrained his desire to attend to all of Katrina's needs? Or, did the relationship come to an end on its own.

As some of you readers probably have experienced, some relationships seem to end on their own, some go on with very little effort. It is difficult for us to know what our partner is going to decide, if he/she is going to do the right thing, if suddenly one day they (or you) decide it's over. I have seen many forms of relationships in my years of spiritual counseling. Some were about sex and one-night stands, some lasted over 50 years, and many are somewhere in-between.

With the divorce rate high it is easy to think that if a relationship doesn't work out, that you will find another, and another. But you cannot escape your own karma, and the result of the decisions you make that affect your life path. Your decisions affect the quality of your character, and thus your personal, familial, parental, social (and more) karma.

As Ralph came to me for consultation and to help him reflect on Katrina's actions and motivations, the "why" question was prominent for another reason. Many times, it is so very difficult for a 2nd chakra dominant person to let go, because of their desire to see things as they could be, as perfect. When someone you love does not do a thing you see that would be beneficial, it partly bothers us because we are invested in the outcome, and partly because we cannot make the decision for the other person as to what's best.

We all have 2nd chakras, so we all experience this to a certain degree, but it can be very difficult to let go of a relationship when you are the one that is still in love! Knowing that Katrina is moving in a different direction has not made it any easier for Ralph to reconcile his understanding of her actions. He may never fully know the "why" of her departure, but it is more important that Ralph focus on his reactions, rather than on what Katrina is thinking. He cannot control her thinking, but he can control how he responds.

That is not to say he should not care, but rather it is important for him (and for Katrina) to be spiritually centered and focused.

Katrina must work on being more grounded, so that she does not overwhelm so easily in a relationship. Katrina should also work on communication, as she may have trusted her feelings in ending the relationship but did not fully communicate the reasons to Ralph (even though she wrote a book on how to go lovingly through relationships that end...perhaps a lesson she needed to learn).

Ralph must stop trying to second-guess Katrina, as painful as it is, and focus on his own integrity (2nd chakra persons must place a value on their "sweetness" as well as be gentle with himself and avoid self-criticism). It is possible the relationship could have ended because it had reached its own fruition; lessons learned, karma complete, or some grander lesson that affected them both for a time.

Some of you may have experienced the same phenomena, where relationships just end of their own accord. I know it is not the same value system our parents have held, where most people who married did so with the intent that it was for life. I believe that such relationships are still very possible.

However, we are under much more stress and distractions than our parents were. There is an acceleration of technology, information exchange, fast-paced living, and a challenge for our ability to keep up with the amount and speed of change in the world today.

It is easy to become overwhelmed and to lose focus by living in the illusory comfort of the material world and possessions. It becomes more imperative that we live balanced, spiritual lives so that we are unaffected by the vast changes around us. As we are centered and focused spiritually, everything else falls into place.

Even so, this is a case history of two spiritually-aware people who still experienced the end of a loving relationship. How we deal with ending a relationship is as much a development of the nature of our character as how we attract and initiate the relationship.

5 and 2
big plans and overwhelm

Doug (5) is a very successful businessman who lives with his wife Sheryl (2) and their two children in the wine country of central California. They are a congenial, outgoing, and hard-working couple who have achieved financial and marital stability.

Sheryl is a larger-than-life, ebullient woman who is very much the 2nd chakra visionary in creating big pictures and then living life in them. Doug is a grounded 5th chakra teacher who is happy with a simple life. Simple, in this context, does not mean simplistic. It means he does not have the big sweeping visions and is content in his "groundedness," is a good father and provider, and is very loving towards his family.

Why is this a case history? I have known and counseled Doug and Sheryl for several years. Doug can be overwhelmed at times by the grandiosity of Sheryl's enthusiastic trust in a larger, fuller picture for their lives together. He wants to please her and help her realize her and their dreams.

Doug's overwhelm can cause a reaction of being ungrounded as he tries to deal with the stress. When a 5th chakra person becomes ungrounded, they can also lose a little (or more) sense of their identity. In fact, I have noticed over the years some similarities in the chakras that when stressed, the individual loses a little of their sense of individuality.

Some people can suffer for years in a form of quiet desperation. They so much desire change in their life but don't know how to accomplish it, or where to start. The soul quality always seeks to externalize, through the personality, the seeds of a greater expression, a more sacred and holy expression, of that person's true character and spiritual quality. Spiritual, when I describe it, pertains to the highest qualities of one's character in God.

For the 2nd chakra person, there oftentimes is no immediate answer because there is not supposed to be one. That means faith and internal trust are the keys for managing those moments in time, moving towards the expression of one's true nature, when it seems the external world and conscious thinking provide no cues as to what's next.

For the 5th chakra person, there may be knowledge of what to do, but perhaps what is the best way to express it (comprehension and meaning) can be very frustrating. After all, clear emotional communication is a very large part of a successful relationship.

But what if your desire to communicate may not be "fully heard" by your partner? What if you two "agree" on something, but still have different ideas of what that is?

Even if the 2nd chakra person trusts their intuition, and the 5th chakra person is very grounded, it does not necessarily mean true communication will take place. There are many other factors involved:

- *Relationship Karma* - There may be a karmic reason why Doug and Sheryl do this dance, time after time, and it seems to escalate to proportions that can lead to overwhelm.
- *Mission Statements* - Each individual must pass beyond their own perceptions and limitations when interacting with their partner, in order to provide the possibility of an even greater depth of relationship.
- *Individual Free Will* - Each of us has a free will that we believe makes us independent of our actions and

independent from others. Yet everything is dependent and in unity. What you decide with your free will is connected to all things. The more awareness (consciousness) you apply to your actions, the more powerful the expression of your true nature.

Remember that it is not just the goal, but the effort that defines one's character in life. Doug and Sheryl may be destined to work on this aspect of their relationship, to varying degrees, for the duration of their marriage. That does not make it good or bad, but provides (always) the opportunity for growth and understanding.

So, after all that, what can Doug do in measure to his 5th chakra's best expression to Sheryl? Being grounded and trusting the feelings he has, should come first.

Emotional communication with Sheryl as to the fears/desires/nuances regarding any subject is going to have the best effect for her, as she is looking to see if Doug is grasping her "big picture." Remember, one of the driving forces of the 2nd chakra is self-acceptance, and that can externalize as a desire to have others acknowledge Sheryl's perceptions of the whole.

And, Doug can remember that even his best explanation of his feelings does not guarantee that Sheryl will understand. It's not about her intellect, it's about two souls united in a marriage who represent the further possibility of awakening each other to their true nature. How they do that is the definition of their character, not the personal interpretation of the goal itself.

And what can Sheryl do? She must trust her intuition to see things as they are, and be receptive to Doug's communications. She must also be comfortable with a little chaos in her life (the misunderstandings) that becomes manageable as she remains in equanimity.

Sheryl can come to realize she cannot make anyone live in the higher perceptions she envisions for them, but that they will eventually get there. She can give up a little control in favor of an understanding guidance based in compassion and harmlessness.

3 and 3
approaching the crossroads

Andrea (3) and Karl (3) have been married for 18 years. They have a special-needs 13-year-old son Daniel (5) who requires a significant amount of attention and assistance.

Andrea came to me, and as in most spiritual consultations, I talked for 15 – 20 minutes without asking questions, revealing what I saw as her dominant chakra, life's strengths and issues, and so on. I do this in part to show that the higher planes of consciousness are real and viable, so as to help the individual see their true spiritual nature.

As I spoke with Andrea, she began to cry as she realized the crossroads she had approached in her life. I saw her husband as a kind and well-meaning man, but a person living more in the lower aspects of his 3rd chakra (self-esteem, self-worth issues). Andrea was living in the higher aspects of her 3rd chakra (strong sense of moral and ethical character). I discussesd with her the metaphor of the two magnets whose north poles were pushing away from each other.

As you know by now, the 3rd chakra individual must work at making emotional decisions that are based on their truth, uniqueness, and power, and that these qualities deal with the development of character.

The reason Andrea must be in this position is that she must decide how best to proceed, for I knew she was questioning her relationship with Karl without her having mentioned it. I gently started the session with an indirect analogy so as to set the stage for the rest of what was to follow about her 3rd chakra character.

Having a 5th chakra dominant special-needs son is very demanding, and I told Andrea about techniques to help him to stay focused, grounded, and in his body. I showed her how to calm his mind and the importance of understanding that 95% of all communication is energy (consciousness).

How could Andrea make the best affect to her marriage and parenting? As Gandhi said: "We must be the change we seek in the world."

The only way that Andrea can truly help her family is by being the essence of her 3rd chakra. That is, the 3rd chakra person is usually driven to look for the essence of "the thing itself."

So, if she finds her inner truth, what if her partner has not found that same level? What if Karl is doing his best? Is that good enough? How can one really know when it is time to change a relationship?

As the spiritual consultation continued, Andrea revealed her emotional confusion and that she had been contemplating ending the relationship with Karl. This presents even more special circumstances, because of the situation with their son, Daniel.

What should Andrea do? How can she honor her spiritual path and her relationship commitments?

I have noticed over the years that many 3rd chakra individuals are also perennial students. They seem to me to be on a lifelong journey of study: I have seen many continually taking a course in school, or a seminar, or some other form of continuing education. Of course, this is not limited to 3rd chakra dominant people!

I told Andrea that it is unlikely that her son Daniel would improve very much in this lifetime, and that he would remain much the same as he is now. The karma and 5th chakra disposition I saw for Daniel sometimes causes a person to live a lifetime with an infirmity. Some karma extends for many lifetimes in a row!

So, how can Andrea best serve herself and her family? As 3rd chakra individuals also ultimately become very spiritual (or fight it for a lifetime), Andrea must live to her convictions as to what she feels is her highest truth. In so doing, she is taking a psychic relationship to what her own soul quality represents, emanating through her most dominant 3rd chakra. Living in that truth does not assure her that anyone around her will benefit, but it does represent the *possibility* of benefit by her good choices.

This is so very hard to do in relationships: wanting the best for others, meaning doing the best for yourself so that you are living your life from a position of strength instead of weakness.

Also, the greater truth Andrea lives in, the fewer peers she may have, but only from the fidelity to her own authenticity and veracity can she truly serve to relieve the karma of her husband and son.

5 and 5
an arranged marriage

William (5) is a gay single male who is very direct, forward-thinking and tough-minded. He has had one major relationship in his life and left his partner some years ago. Certainly impatient in most of his endeavors, he is nonetheless very gentle on the inside.

Ivana (5) is a divorced heterosexual mother of two who came to the U.S. after her separation. In order for Ivana to gain citizenship, she paid William a rather large sum of money to "marry" her.

Ivana has an alcohol and smoking problem, and her children (in their early teens) are being affected by her behavior. Ivana's divorce left her with a considerable amount of money, so she does not need to work, and spoils the children with material goods, yet is not seeing to their true emotional needs. It was a small matter for her to pay William for the benefit of citizenship.

William and Ivana live in separate houses and the children live solely with Ivana. William will take the children to some functions and go shopping with Ivana from time to time, but that is the extent of their relationship.

William is quite astute, and in his direct manner has taken the two children under his wing and is parenting them as best he can, though he has no interest in being a father. It is an interesting situation, for though he feigns interest, he deeply cares about the two children and is frustrated at the effect Ivana's self-destructive behavior is having on her children. William has had "heart-to-heart" talks with Ivana, but she often becomes cavalier and disdainful, refusing to see the downhill path her children are on.

William does what he can, realizes he is not the children's father, and intercedes in their welfare by abruptly bringing situations to Ivana's attention when he can stand no more.

This confrontational relationship has been quite the struggle for William, as he sees futility in his desire to help the children, and he also sees no effort on Ivana's part to improve herself. Her occasional drinking binges have a deleterious effect on the children as she becomes belligerent and vocally abusive, and she only becomes coherent after several days of drinking. As William sees this behavior clearly, his direct manner desires her to face reality and change before the damage to her children's development becomes even more severe.

The children see the goodness in William's sometimes gruff demeanor: they are able to look past his glare and see the tenderness and concern beneath. Ivana seems to be in a continuing cycle, partly due to her wealth giving her so many more options to behave the way she does without any seeming consequences.

Here, Ivana is living that classical lower aspect of the 5th chakra in seeking the drinking and smoking that will help take her out-of-body and thus help numb the feelings of the physical plane of existence. She is choosing to relate to William's 5th chakra as little as possible, ignoring or denying her telepathy that she drew him into her life as much more than a husband of convenience: he is a direct wake-up call.

William, on the other hand, has had to deal with several hardships in life that grounded him in the physical plane. He understands those hardships and chooses to meet them head on. What Ivana's 5th chakra offers to William is what can happen when one tries to stay out of body. This has the effect of only angering William regarding Ivana's behavior, and causes him frustration that he cannot explain (as 5th chakra does) the meaning and consequences of her actions.

When two 5th chakra people are relating to each other, the goal of increasing the level of understanding is a deep, foundational motivation for the consciousness of the individual.

In this case, both William and Ivana are very strong personalities with 5th chakra dominances. This relationship shows many aspects of the 5th chakra:

- The desire for direct communication
- One partner who is emotionally unavailable (William) by choice, due to the marriage of convenience (the money he was paid), his sexual preference, and his disdain for Ivana's attitude.
- One partner who is emotionally unavailable (Ivana) by choice, by being cavalier about life, and resorting to smoking/drinking to leave her body as much as possible, thus emotionally abandoning her children, and assuaging their feelings by buying them material things.
- William is a grounded 5th chakra and is very stable emotionally.
- Ivana is an ungrounded 5th chakra and is emotionally unstable.

One of the lessons the 5th chakra individual learns is when to let go of trying to explain something to someone who is not yet ready to learn. If another person is not capable or ready to learn, the patience of a saint will not increase the other person's understanding.

At this point, after reading these case histories, you can perceive the complexities and difficulties that ensue when the human psyche grapples with levels of awareness.

Of course, the whole idea is that increasing consciousness (being aware that you are aware) will overcome the illusion of separation and thus overcome the suffering that goes with it.

Would you now consider that between people, in their chosen relationships, there is an eloquent lesson deep within their being, co-created by them, that is designed to bless and emancipate them from suffering?

Would you now think that *you* are co-creating at this very moment, eloquent lessons in your own life, that offer you the same gift?

SUMMARY OF THE BOOK

As you can see from reading the case histories, it can be a bit overwhelming to consider all the complex nuances of the chakra's influence on our perceptions, and thus our will/reactions. And these examples only reflect a small part of the greater dynamics that occur between us at the subtle level in relationships. It is the tip of the iceberg of who we really are.

All the chakras are working together, but a dominant chakra emphasizes the tendencies that form our perspective of the world and our associations, and the unfolding of our consciousness in the sea of the human condition.

It makes the case for each of us to seek our own center of peace and calmness, and to nurture and cultivate our own spiritual evolution and balance. Much of that balance will reflect back to us in our various chakra relationships.

You may have observed in these case histories some past life information. I thought it important for you to read about it because this life's experience is not our only one, and the gem that is us has many facets on which the light reflects differently.

We all recapitulate (bring forward) the qualities of our several past life experiences. Be mindful of what you create in this lifetime: you may bring it forward in a future one.

As you evolve, you separate yourself from ignorance and the limitations of linear thinking. You become an equal participant in both higher awareness and the rational mind.

Improving yourself and arising in your own consciousness is the best way you can help others, especially in your relationships.

May you always stay in balance, and lead a life of love, compassion, and harmlessness.

ABOUT THE AUTHOR

For 18 years Dr. Richard Jelusich has been of service as a renowned spiritual counselor, healer, author, and international lecturer, blending Western science and Eastern philosophy to de-mystify metaphysics.

His Ph.D. in Human Science is from the California Institute for Human Science (CIHS), where he is a former Dean of Administration and current core faculty professor, and serves on the board of directors. He has been an ordained reverend since 1995 through the Universal Church of the Master, Santa Clara, CA.

A gifted psychic from birth, Dr. Jelusich's mission is to heal and self-empower the "whole human being" on all four levels of daily life—*mental, physical, emotional,* and *spiritual.* He provides enlightenment and practical tools to recognize our multi-dimensional, metaphysical nature.

He offers a number of metaphysical and spiritual services, including: one-on-one counseling; a 17-level *Healer's Training Course* taught throughout the US and Canada; *Light News, Inc.* publications and books; meditation CD's; and an annual guided tour to study Maya cosmology in Central America. He has travelled to Canada, Central America, Europe and Japan to present lectures, workshops, spiritual practices.

Dr. Jelusich's technical background includes a high-level engineering, management and consulting career in space launch systems with NASA, General Dynamics and other aerospace corporations. He was also Configuration and Data Manager for the

Advanced Systems Division of United Technologies. *(M.S., Systems Management, 1987, University of Southern California, CA; Certified Manufacturing Engineer (C.MFg.E.) 1984, Society of Manufacturing Engineers; B.S., Business Management, 1977, San Diego State University, CA)*

He followed his heart's desire to study behavioral psychoacoustics, cymatics, bio-electromagnetics, clinical biopsychology, consciousness expansion, trans-personal psychology, and Eastern-Western philosophy. Dr. Jelusich's Ph.D. dissertation is: *"Psychophysiological Effects of Frequency Octave Related Light and Sound."*

Dr. Jelusich produced 22 public-access television shows of "Metaphysics 101" on the mind-body-spirit connection. He has been featured on numerous radio programs, and as keynote speaker/lecturer for the Universal Church of the Master annual convention, IONS (Institute for Noetic Sciences), and at holistic health expos, conventions, national healings, and other prominent metaphysical events.

Dr. Jelusich's private counseling sessions determine your soul's purpose, with the focus on self-empowerment. As an intuitive counselor, his ability to "see" the subtle energies in and around our bodies and chakras enables him to discern life path strengths and weaknesses to help us understand and integrate our life issues.

He has facilitated the healing of thousands worldwide through spiritual consultations, "Flower Readings," meditation groups, and workshops, and has received many testimonials on the profound effects of his healing abilities.

Courses & Seminars Offered by Dr. Jelusich
(See page 218 for contact/schedule info)

Healer's Training Course for the Whole Human Being
Dr. Jelusich travels throughout the U.S. and Canada teaching his 17-level, 2-year *Healer's Training Course* in spiritual healing and philosophy of being. Healers-in-training learn various healing methods, techniques, and philosophy in an experiential, hands-on environment under Dr. Jelusich's direction. *Please request an information packet.*

Psychology of the Chakras
Based on Dr. Jelusich's popular book <u>Eye of the Lotus: Psychology of the Chakras,</u> this is an esoteric look at the philosophy and psychology of being and how chakras affect mental, spiritual, emotional and physical aspects of your life. Includes practical advice on chakra balancing and toning exercises, prayers, meditations, yoga, oils, etc.

I Can Relate
A powerful workshop in understanding the subtle energy connections between people in relationships, based on dominant chakras. The presentation includes audience interactive participation, and secrets to determine your own and others' dominant chakra.

The Healing Power of Sound and Light
A popular multi-media, multi-sensory presentation on the integration of light, sound, and form for healing the mind and body, based on the science of psychoacoustics and cymatics.

Maya Path to 2012
What did the Mayan culture understand of the evolution/acceleration of consciousness, advanced astronomy, and the natural frequencies of time/space? The presentation is based in part on the annual trips Dr. Jelusich leads to the Yucatan and Guatemala to study Maya cosmology.

Past Lives, Karma, and Reincarnation
An investigative, philosophical, and intuitively experiential lecture on karma and reincarnation relative to your current life.

The Energetic Connection: For Dentists and Hygienists
"What really happens between you and your patient, energetically?" Blending science and Eastern philosophy, this presentation provides useful techniques and exercises for maintaining healthy boundaries, regenerating the Self, and how to soothe the patient.

De-Mystifying Metaphysics
The subject of metaphysics is difficult to understand because it cannot be observed directly with any of the five senses. Yet it exists, as science is now proving what mystics have known for thousands of years.

Healing Technologies for the New Millennium
New devices are being created that measure the subtle energy in the meridians, the level of awakening of the chakras, and the aura of the human body. Dr. Jelusich explores what these healing devices are and how they work.

Embracing the Feminine Principle
Most people are not familiar with this principle, or its emergence at this time in the evolution of our consciousness. This presentation explains the Feminine Principle and how it uses the power of the will to allow each person's, male or female, spiritual growth.

Sacred Geometries
Specific geometric relationships, found throughout nature, have been called "sacred" because they represent the fundamental organizing principle that conscious human beings understand in the universe. Dr. Jelusich will explain these geometries and give light and sound demonstrations of their innate properties and beauty.

Experiential Healing, the Integration of Self
Based on the popular "Healers Training for the Whole Human Being," this presentation covers "Qualitative Healing," the most powerful form of spiritual healing Dr. Jelusich has discovered. The lecture covers the philosophy of spiritual healing not limited to time or space, and may involve audience participation.

Services Offered by Dr. Jelusich
(See page 218 for contact/schedule info)

FLOWER READINGS
A popular small, fun, group format for conveying the reality of our active, yet often dormant intuition. Dr. Jelusich intuitively "reads" each individual's flower anonymously, conveying dominant chakra strengths, weaknesses, and current life issues. Information is given respectfully in the group setting, and is recorded on a CD.

PRIVATE SESSIONS
Private consultations seek to determine your soul's purpose in this lifetime. They are conducted with Dr. Jelusich's direct intuitive perceptions of a person's individual character, life disposition, and functioning of the chakras and body systems. Sessions are a combination of intuitive counseling and energy work, in-person or by phone, and are recorded for you on CD.

GUIDED MEDITATIONS
Meditating as a group with unanimity of purpose promotes more rapid upward evolution of the soul, in a place of peace and safety. This type of meditation uses live or recorded music, and guided imagery. Also, full moon, puja, solstice, and equinox meditations can be scheduled.

COURSES THROUGH CALIFORNIA INSTITUTE FOR HUMAN SCIENCE (CIHS)
Dr. Jelusich teaches several courses on campus and online, including:

- Psychology of the Chakras: a 4-unit class based on his book, <u>Eye of the Lotus</u>.
- Karma and Reincarnation
- Toward a Superconsciousness
- Spirituality and Consciousness

Contact info:

California Institute for Human Science: 760-634-1771
701 Garden View Court, Encinitas, CA 92024
or www.cihs.edu

GUIDED TOUR SERIES: "MAYA PATH TO 2012"

Dr. Jelusich has been leading yearly guided spiritual journeys (open to the public) to study Maya Cosmology in Central America since 2005, and will do so until 2017. He teams up with Dr. Miguel Angel Vergara.

Dr. Vergara focuses on sacred ceremonies, the deeper esoteric meanings of Maya teachings, and the roots of the Maya prophecies for 2012. Dr. Jelusich focuses on Maya cosmology, astronomy, the acceleration of time/consciousness, and the relationship of our solar system to the Galactic Center.

Each year's journey focuses on different sacred sites in the Yucatan and Guatemala, and includes visits to those sites, day and evening lectures, meditations and much more. These trips are designed for those who wish a more serious study of the Mayan consciousness and cosmology.

As the years towards 2012 become fewer, it is ever more important to understand our cosmology. Learn first-hand about the Maya's deep understanding of our spiritual nature, and the movement of the Earth, Solar System and the Galactic Mother (Center of our Galaxy).

Contact info:

Sacred Earth Journeys: toll free 877-874-7922
Suite 220 – 133 E. 8th Ave
Vancouver, BC, V5T 1R8 Canada
or www.sacredearthjourneys.ca

EYE OF THE LOTUS:
Psychology of the Chakras
(See page 218 for ordering information)

An extremely practical handbook to take control of your life and to understand subtle energy consciousness. This is new and valuable information that bridges the traditional yoga teachings of India on the chakras, with powerful modern psychological techniques suitable for our needs in the present day world. A spiritual handbook of tremendous scope and power.

Published by Lotus Press and now in its second printing, Eye of the Lotus: *Psychology of the Chakras*, is a comprehensive guide on how our chakras (energy centers) affect our mental, physical, spiritual, and emotional states of being. Chakras are our access to our higher selves, and each uniquely affects our nature and disposition.

Dr. Jelusich provides insight and practical techniques for self-empowerment, balance, and harmony, such as hatha yoga techniques for toning and balancing the chakras, meditations and prayers, essential oils, sounds that heal the chakras, and much more.

CRYSTAL BOWLS OF TIBET CD
Healing Sounds for Mind, Body, and Spirit
Dr. Jacob Hans and Dr. Richard Jelusich

(See page 218 for ordering information)

Listen to the meditative, relaxing, and healing sounds of quartz crystal bowls. Each track varies from one bowl played alone -- to sequences of several bowls played together -- creating beautiful, overlapping, harmonious sound patterns.

Crystal bowls are known for their pure sound, and are used in healing and energy clearing with very good results.

Using a unique recording method, seven crystal bowls of varying sizes were positioned in a circle, with special microphones in the center to capture the overlapping, resonating sound patterns from different directions. The listening experience is as close to 3-D as possible.

Listening to this CD with headphones will accurately reproduce the sound patterns and crystal bowl orientation. Listening with stereo speakers will bath the room with an excellent bass response and incredible cascading sounds.

Schedule...
COUNSELING SESSIONS and LECTURES
Toll free: **877-CHAKRA1 (877-242-5721)**
International: **760-420-8100**
E-mail: **info@lightnews.org**

—ᴍ—

Order...
BOOKS and CDs
Toll free: **877-CHAKRA1 (877-242-5721)**
International: **760-420-8100**
www.lightnews.org or E-mail: **info@lightnews.org**

—ᴍ—

Sign up for...
"LIGHT NEWS" E-mail newsmagazine
An E-mail newsmagazine dedicated
to the blending of science and metaphysics,
published monthly in the U.S. and Canada.
Light News is also available on Dr. Jelusich's website.
www.lightnews.org
Light News website offers a wealth of information,
including Dr. Jelusich's schedule of events, collection of writings,
spiritual services, products, links, and much more.

—ᴍ—

Contact...
THE AUTHOR
Richard Jelusich, Ph.D.
P.O. Box 17035, San Diego, CA 92177
E-mail: **info@lightnews.org**